Venus Signs

About the Author

Jessica Shepherd is an astrologer, writer, and health coach who specializes in counseling people through personal growth and awakening. Jessica believes astrology can help us understand ourselves and our relationships, and even guide us to make better decisions. Author of *A Love Alchemist's Notebook: Magical Secrets for Drawing Your True Love into Your Life* (Llewellyn, 2010) and *Karmic Dates & Momentary Mates: The Astrology of the Fifth House* (Moonkissd, 2014), Jessica has studied astrology since 1992 and practiced astrology professionally since 2003. She holds a BA in Arts Management from Coastal Carolina University (Conway, SC) and is a graduate of Steven Forrest's Evolutionary Astrology Apprenticeship program.

As a certified health coach (CHC), Jessica specializes in clean eating, the mind-body connection, and stress and chronic illness management. Find out more about Jessica's health coaching services at www.jessicashepherd.net. To read more of Jessica's astrology writings, visit her astrology blog at www.moonkissd.com.

Jessica loves fan mail! You can write to her at Moonkissd@moonkissd.com.

JESSICA SHEPHERD

Venus Signs

Discover Your
Erotic Gifts and *Secret Desires*
Through Astrology

Llewellyn Publications
Woodbury, Minnesota

FIRST EDITION
First Printing, 2015

Cover art: iStockphoto.com/5888684/©cidepix,
    iStockphoto.com/11897627/©CT757fan
Cover design by Lisa Novak
Editing by Andrea Neff

Llewellyn Publications is a registered trademark of Llewellyn Worldwide Ltd.

Library of Congress Cataloging-in-Publication Data

Shepherd, Jessica, 1973–
  Venus signs : discover your erotic gifts & secret desires through
astrology / by Jessica Shepherd. — First edition.
      pages   cm
  Includes bibliographical references.
  ISBN 978-0-7387-4194-9
  1. Venus (Planet)—Miscellanea. 2. Astrology. I. Title.
  BF1724.2.V45S54 2015
  133.5'34—dc23
                                                          2014032581

Llewellyn Worldwide Ltd. does not participate in, endorse, or have any authority or responsibility concerning private business transactions between our authors and the public.
  All mail addressed to the author is forwarded but the publisher cannot, unless specifically instructed by the author, give out an address or phone number.
  Any Internet references contained in this work are current at publication time, but the publisher cannot guarantee that a specific location will continue to be maintained. Please refer to the publisher's website for links to authors' websites and other sources.

Llewellyn Publications
A Division of Llewellyn Worldwide Ltd.
2143 Wooddale Drive
Woodbury, MN 55125-2989
www.llewellyn.com

Printed in the United States of America

ALSO BY JESSICA SHEPHERD

A Love Alchemist's Notebook: Magical Secrets
for Drawing Your True Love into Your Life
(Llewellyn, 2010)

Karmic Dates and Momentary Mates:
The Astrology of the Fifth House
(Moonkissd, 2014)

This book is dedicated to my best friend and sister, Erika, for her compassion, strength, support, and unconditional love.

ACKNOWLEDGMENTS

I am indebted to so many in ways that transcend words, but I will try.

Steven Forrest and Paul Bogle, astrology mentors extraordinaire, for the master astrological teachings each has imparted. The confidence these men place in me continues to give me confidence in myself.

Holiday Mathis, astrologer, ally, and creative partner whose mega-watt brilliance inspired me to actually *write* my first book.

April Elliot Kent, astrologer extraordinaire, whose years of webmaster, art, and enthusiastic professional support have evolved into a golden friendship.

My family: Erika and James Everett, and new niece Ella Rae. My stepdaughters, Hewson, Maggie, and Sarah, and their father and my husband, John Shepherd. All of you open my heart wider. Sun, I love you to the Moon and back.

Cherished friends and allies: Fern Feto Spring, Emma Rigge, Claire Skougor, Jonathan Pearl, Grant Jeffers, Jeff Kishner, Jeremy Neal, and Minouche Graglia. And to my early book reviewers who gave me invaluable feedback: Toni Piccinini, Lise Castro, Marian Husband, and Cynthia Tracy. Thank you.

Erin Reese, initial editor and creative midwife, for her friendship, unflagging cheerleading, and belief in my work.

Finally, gratitude to Venus, the Great Goddess who invisibly inspires all creative acts of love and magic, and all teachers, in body and spirit form. If I know one thing for sure, it's that we are never alone.

CONTENTS

Introduction . . . 1

Your Astrological Venus Sign . . . 5

Venus in Aries . . . 11

Venus in Taurus . . . 27

Venus in Gemini . . . 43

Venus in Cancer . . . 57

Venus in Leo . . . 73

Venus in Virgo . . . 87

Venus in Libra . . . 103

Venus in Scorpio . . . 117

Venus in Sagittarius . . . 133

Venus in Capricorn . . . 147

Venus in Aquarius . . . 163

Venus in Pisces . . . 179

Conclusion . . . 195
For Further Understanding . . . 199
Appendix 1: Good Witch, Bad Witch . . . 201
Appendix 2: Venus Tables, 1950 to 2020 . . . 209

Introduction

Venus is the goddess of love, relationships, and pleasure. Coveted throughout the ages, she embodies the sweetness we seek in life: connection, joy, romance, abundance, and pleasure. Inspiring connection and then the magic that keeps us together, she answers the questions: What qualities do I most value in a partner? What is the special magnetism I have that makes me desirable to others? What do I most need in a partner and best friend, and what qualities can I cultivate to connect with them? What turns me on? What will keep my long-term relationship humming along happily forever? The answers to these questions are individual and unique to you.

We each have a particular set of erotic desires, likes, loves, and preferred ways of connecting with everything and everyone we love—that's our Venus sign. You may be familiar with your astrological Sun sign, but your Sun sign is often not the same as your Venus sign. While your Sun sign speaks to your basic character motivations, your Venus sign speaks to your relationship motivations and style, how you connect to others, who and what you find attractive, and what you need to keep romance strong in a committed partnership. Likewise, when determining

romantic compatibility, Venus sign comparisons are far more reliable than those of Sun signs.

In this book, you will discover the secret desires, love charms,
erotic gifts, and shadow qualities inherent to your specific Venus
sign. But before you proceed, you may wish to know the basic
nuts and bolts of the astrological Venus.

Each astrological planet represents a specific quality of energy in our lives, and the planet Venus holds the impulse of *eros*,
or erotic desire. Erotic desire isn't strictly sexual; it's a quality
of receptive magnetism that draws to us what and whom we
love—people, pleasure, beauty, joy, and abundance. Pleasure is
fulfilling, but it's also often a means to achieving Venus's main
goal: making a connection. When we say to someone "I can
relate," we're connecting through Venus's empathy and understanding, two of the most precious Venus gifts in the world.
When we share similar tastes, interests, aesthetics, joys, and
pleasures, we connect, and when these preferences are harmo-
nious, we experience the romance and magic of love—or at
least the potential for it.

The Mythical Venus

In ancient myth, Venus was known as the pleasure-loving goddess. She could always be found where people were laughing
and having a good time, making merry at taverns and weddings, brothels and dress shops, art salons, lavish dinner parties,
and behind the closed doors of bedrooms. You may remember learning in school about the Roman Venus or her Greek
counterpart, Aphrodite, the coveted beauty who swaggered
through mythology books with erotic confidence, panache,
and a magic girdle, starting love affairs, catfights, and wars.
In fact, at the heart of every civilization there was a woman

coveted for her magic, artistry, fertility, emotional/social intelligence, and beauty. Inanna (Sumeria), Ishtar (Babylon), Astarte (Phoenicia), and Isis (Egypt) are all synonymous with the beautiful and sometimes fierce archetype we call Venus. Venus's myths always intrigue and fascinate us because they resemble our own lives. Who hasn't known a woman (or been that woman) who had to wrest her power back from others? Who among us hasn't dreamt of donning a magic girdle that makes people swoon, or saying "damn the consequences" and courageously going after who and what we love?

THE APHRODITE ARCHETYPE

We all have a Venus sign, but for some people, Aphrodite/Venus guides almost every area of their lives with her invisible hand. According to Jean Shinoda Bolen in her book *Goddesses in Everywoman*, for an Aphrodite-identified woman, relationships between things, ideas, and people are all-important. Sexually independent yet craving emotional involvement, an Aphrodite-identified woman can be in a committed relationship but generally feels comfortable when she is involved in a variety of relationships and extramarital affairs. A muse or artist herself, she is attracted to creative types who mirror her drive to create; her role is to inspire. She may or may not be classically beautiful, but she has a magnetism that attracts both sexes. And as any Aphrodite-identified woman knows, great beauty is both a blessing and a curse: she often wonders whether she is loved and valued for who she is or for who she is to others. Marilyn Monroe was a tragic example of an Aphrodite-identified woman.

VENUS DISPOSSESSION

Like a diamond, Venus shimmers with the promise of fulfillment, love, and happiness. Unfortunately, there's often a vast gulf between Venus's promise of sunsets and magic and our experience of her in our lives. Look at the number of people consulting astrologers, life coaches, and therapists because they want more love, happiness, money, confidence, and passion. These are all Venus problems. Venus is available to everyone, but for many, she has been tainted by media messages, misunderstandings, aging, and mother complexes. I first heard about Venus dispossession from astrologer Dana Gerhardt, who described giving up on being a girl when her sister was given the beauty in the family and she the brains. Venus dispossession is an apt term for a common phenomenon. Negative messages from our culture, media, church, and family about our beauty and our bodies, unhealed sexual abuse, partners who are abusive or critical—all of these can cause us to make harsh judgments about our feminine eroticism, beauty, and value as individuals. However, we can awaken the joyful, uninhibited, abundance-loving temptress we call Aphrodite at any time—through our Venus sign.

Your Astrological Venus Sign

*Venus reflects a fundamental need within us to challenge
those social and moral restrictions which we impose
upon our hearts for the sake of safety and respectability,
and draws us instead into relationships which connect us
with an immediate, passionate and vivid sense of life.*

~LIZ GREENE, ASTROLOGER

There are twelve signs in astrology, from Aries to Pisces, each
of which belongs to a constellation. At the time of your birth,
Venus was traveling through one of these twelve signs. You
can use the Venus tables (appendix 2) at the end of this book to
find your Venus sign.

Your Venus sign illuminates your feminine side, your empathic, receptive, sensual self who values harmony, pleasure,
relaxation, and connection. Your Venus sign reveals how you
express sensuality and what (and whom) you desire, enjoy, and
find beautiful. It also describes how you connect emotionally
with others and what prevents this connection from happening.

Your Venus sign reveals how you approach relationships and
what you want most from your significant partners, lovers, and

friends. Are you excited by the thrill of a conquest, and once in a relationship, can you be competitive, impatient, or impulsive (Venus in Aries)? Are you attracted to socially sophisticated, graceful, and intelligent partners, and do your relationships bring out your tendency to try to make everyone else happy (Venus in Libra)? Or are you drawn toward emotionally intense partners, and do you often find it hard to let go, forgive, and move on from a disagreement or person (Venus in Scorpio)?

If you've experienced the phenomenon of losing your head to love, you've learned that we humans are not always conscious or in control of our affinities and desires. We may be attracted to a certain person or activity but not understand why. The people, ideas, activities, things, and pleasures to which you are magnetically drawn mirror your deepest desires, even if they challenge your conscious choices, your self-image, and your comfort zone. They may shake you up and confuse and unsettle you—and ultimately help you to know yourself better.

Our Venus sign tells us what is non-negotiable in our soulmates—the most enduring relationships of our lives. Do you find it impossible to form partnerships with those who lack open-mindedness and curiosity (Venus in Gemini)? Are compassion, nurturing tenderness, and emotional empathy and support absolute must-haves in your closest relationships (Venus in Cancer)? Our Venus sign describes our deepest relationship values as well as our relationship deal breakers—qualities we do without only at great cost to our emotional happiness.

Our Venus sign inspires the sparks of love, and then works to keep love alive. During the falling-in-love phase, pheromones are on tap, but sustaining romance requires our conscious awareness and participation. Between family and household roles and obligations, it's all too easy to lose touch with the magic in committed partnerships. The mythical Venus never underestimated the rejuvenating power of pleasure, and neither should we. By nurturing the joys of our respective Venus signs, we rejuvenate our partnerships as well as the feminine wellspring in ourselves.

VENUS: YOUR FAIRY GODMOTHER OR AN EVIL QUEEN?

Venus can be our sacred ally and fairy godmother, leading us to deep and lasting fulfillment, but she can also be an evil queen, a force of disconnection and misery. Every Venus sign has its own set of fairy godmother and evil queen behaviors. Astrologers call these the "light" and "shadow" sides of each sign.

The fairy godmother is powerfully centered in her feminine wisdom and knows how to be generous with others while making her own happiness central. She honors her needs, desires, and wants by asking for them and then following through. When someone counters her desires, she negotiates, because she knows that finding a way to meet her needs and desires is an act of self-respect. She takes her desire for pleasure, joy, and satisfaction seriously.

The evil queen looks outside of herself, to others, for approval. She wants everyone to like her and manipulates situations to her advantage. Rather than asking for what she wants, she makes demands and punishes others when she doesn't get her way, as if expecting others to read her mind and know what she desires. The evil queen projects her beauty and power onto others, coveting these qualities; I call this "Venus envy."

Ironically, our shadow-y behavior is motivated by the same thing as our light behavior: the desire for love. But instead of creating connection and affection, the shadow fosters disconnection and disappointment. The good news is that we can choose a different strategy by inviting the fairy godmother into our lives and consciousness, where she can more elegantly rule our relationships, free from the shadows of insecurity and discontent. When we do this, the shadow behaviors of the evil queen are automatically negated, because it is impossible to do both types of behavior at once. Dark Venus is simply absence-of-light Venus, so the more conscious we are of the dark, the freer we are to live in the light.

The light and shadow sides of Venus are explored at length in each Venus sign chapter, but you may also enjoy turning to appendix 1 at the back of this book for a Good Witch/Bad Witch summary of all twelve Venus signs.

VENUS AND THE SUN

As you identify your Venus sign and those of your friends and partners, you may notice a pattern: Venus will always be within two signs preceding or following your Sun sign. This is because Venus rarely travels farther than 45 degrees from the Sun, and each zodiac sign contains 30 degrees. Therefore, since your Venus sign will always be within 45 degrees of the degree of your natal Sun, Venus will never be farther than two zodiac signs away from your Sun.

Just as the planet Venus travels her circular path snugly near the Sun (your Self) in the sky, your Venus sign illuminates what you want most from partnerships. Venus inspires your Sun sign, your creative identity, to create, love, and laugh. Urging you to embody the strengths, ideas, goals, and visions inherent to your Sun sign through play, partnering, art, beauty, inspiration, and pleasure, Venus sees life itself as exciting, a playground full of endless opportunities to love and laugh, to create more inspired beauty and connection in your life.

In summary, your Venus sign describes:

- the unique motives and behaviors of your Venus.
- who and what you enjoy and find attractive and beautiful.
- people, ideas, things, and desires that inspire happiness and pleasure—and that may challenge your comfort zone.
- the special magic you have that reinvigorates romantic and emotional connections.
- your receptive, sensual, feminine side.
- the qualities you value most and must have in a lifelong mate.
- how you emotionally connect to others, ideas, and things.
- your shadow behaviors that block connection.

Here are a few other things you might want to know about your Venus sign. Although these topics are not covered in this book, they can help to further clarify your experience of self-worth, sensual pleasure, and partnership.

Venus House Placement

The house placement of your Venus tells you where you can honor Venus and bring more joy, pleasure, happiness, beauty, and art into your life.

Venus Aspects

Aspects that other planets make to your Venus will subtly or dramatically color the expression of your Venus.

Venus Terms

The Egyptian "terms" pre-date astrological aspects, which are so central to modern astrology. Terms are rarely employed in modern astrology, but according to traditional astrologers, an astrological term flavors the expression of a zodiac sign. How do terms work? Each thirty-degree zodiac sign is chunked, and each division is assigned a planet. For instance, if your Venus is in Mars's term, your love style includes a dash of daring.

Venus Retrograde

Every one and a half years for approximately forty days and nights, Venus appears to move backwards (retrograde) from the earth's perspective. If you were born while Venus was moving retrograde, everything you read about your Venus sign still applies to you, with the caveat that your Venus approaches social conventions, style, art, and relationships in unconventional or extraordinary ways. For instance, Kate Middleton (Venus in Aquarius, retrograde) is known to wear and be photographed in the same gown at many social functions, eschewing popular custom. Your ideas about relationships may be quite different from the prevailing views, as was the case for Brigham Young (Venus in Sagittarius, retrograde), who practiced polygamy. To find out if your Venus is retrograde, visit sasstrology.com or astro.com and enter your birth data. Look for the Venus glyph (♀). If you see an "r" or "Rx" after Venus, you have Venus retrograde.

To find out more about your Venus or other aspects of your birth chart, check out the "For Further Understanding" section at the back of this book.

Venus in Aries
♈

*People, even more than things, have to be restored, renewed,
revived, reclaimed, and redeemed. Never throw out anyone.*

~AUDREY HEPBURN, VENUS IN ARIES

YOUR LOVE ELEMENT

Hot, brazen, passionate fire was once the most coveted element
in the world. The discovery of fire transformed and improved
our lives, but fire is also dangerous. Anyone living in Southern
California knows the devastating power of fire. All it takes is
one small flame, a cigarette carelessly flicked on dry leaves, to
destroy life. On a too-dry day, fire consumes, using everything
in its path as fuel for its insatiable appetite. Controlled burns
are often implemented to preempt the destruction of seasonal
forest fires, as when fire's passions and desires go unchecked,
fire can become deadly, unintentionally burning the very
things that keep it alive. Fire's wisdom teaches the discipline of
regularly harnessing your high-octane strength and channeling

it. By consciously submitting your difficult emotions and desires to a slow burn, you are cleansed and renewed.

Your Secret Desire

A world without passion, adventure, and excitement can get a Venus-in-Aries gal into hot water faster than you can say Robert Downey Jr. (in his days of errant youth). He learned about this Venus's secret desire the hard way, so you don't have to. Instead of inviting unwanted drama and conflict into your love life, you can courageously, consciously, and intentionally court adventure. Harness the power of your passion and charisma, and then get out there and share it with the world!

Your Love Charms

- Your honesty. Others may not want to hear it, but you have the courage not to please others, should you please. You can say what needs to be said, even if it makes you unpopular.

- Your diamond-in-the-rough independence. Your uncut charm endears you to others, while your ballsy attitude lets them know you're your own agent.

- Your daring and bravado. The riskier you play it up, the more attractive you become. On a first date, you list your most dangerous feats: smoking in the bathroom in high school, speeding down the autobahn in Germany, playing your first live gig with your band. You share your exploits not for the accolades but because you take great pleasure in feeling thrillingly alive.

- Your unapologetic insistence on your own rightness (even when you're wrong). When you're not pissing people off, they admire your inspired connection to all things feisty, bold, and alive.

- Your sass. You have a wickedly delicious, cutting sense of humor.

- Your relationship resiliency. You have an EMT-like ability to heal a broken heart or jump-start a broken relationship by diving right back into love, over and over again.

YOUR LOVE GODDESS

Audrey Hepburn (1929–1993) is your Venus-in-Aries goddess. Expressing through Aries, Audrey embodied the beauty and peacemaking urges of Venus. She was a fashion pioneer who launched her own signature style that we admire to this day. She was a freedom fighter and a humanitarian activist who in later years devoted her time to UNICEF, with her belief that every child should have a fighting chance to thrive. Audrey captured our hearts, and we were hooked. We fell in love with her irrepressible, fun-loving enthusiasm, her "funny face," and her moxie—that force of determination, character, and raw nerve. These are qualities that belong to every Venus in Aries.

Audrey did all of this so gracefully. While most of us know her as an actress, a style icon, and, in her later years, a courageous activist for human rights, fewer still know she spent her formative years in conflict, danger, and war. Trained as a ballet dancer as a child, she was thrown headlong into the center of World War II in her early life. This elegant and courageous young ballerina danced for armed soldiers of questionable loyalties as war raged around her. She danced with danger, courageously and gracefully. How apt for Venus, the planet of the arts and relaxation, expressing through Aries, the sign of passion and war.

Aries is the first sign of the zodiac, heralding fiery new beginnings and maverick impulses (like war), as well as the courage to carry them out. In traditional astrology, willful, impetuous, and aggressive Aries was seen as detrimental to Aphrodite, inhibiting her sweetness and her love for harmony and mutual orientation. Astrologer Ronnie Gale Dreyer suggests this is because the ancient Greeks considered Aphrodite's sweetness, beauty, and diplomacy to be traits belonging to the ideal woman, while they derided her independent, passionate, stubborn, and manipulative side. This paradigm is certainly still alive today in our patriarchal culture, as independent-minded, outspoken women who think and act for themselves are often called "bitchy"—or worse.

Aries may not bring out Venus's flowery, soft, and delicate side, but it certainly does bring out the warrior in her. Ferocity, passion, assertiveness, and the ability to go after what she wants are qualities that belong to Venus in Aries. These were also traits admired by people in earlier civilizations who worshiped Venus as Freya (Norse), Inanna (Sumeria), and Ishtar (Babylonia)—civilizations that prized warriors. Likewise, some of this Venus sign's greatest challenges arise from a need to balance her self-concern with consideration for others and the relationship itself. This doesn't mean she is doomed to a life alone, but Venus in Aries does find it all too easy to sever relationship ties and start over, when instead she could learn how to rejuvenate and renew the bond.

Venus in Aries may enjoy thinking of herself as a modern-day Xena warrior princess or similar action heroine. What qualities make a great warrior? Warriors need the ability to face their greatest fears, such as death or defeat in battle. Whether engaging in battle or acting in front of a camera, warriors demonstrate nerve, character, and courage. But Venus in Aries must be more than a warrior; she must become *a warrior of love*. A love warrior learns to be relentlessly honest about her fears, because without emotional honesty, she finds it difficult to trust. A warrior of love learns to honestly confront problems in her partnership instead of blasting someone with pent-up dissatisfaction or allowing ongoing frustration to chip away at happiness. A warrior of love knows that we all disagree at times and we must learn to keep the peace by developing strategies for fighting fair. Venus in Aries has signed up to bravely face her own stuff in relationships—the good, the bad, and the ugly. This will probably involve intense discussions and some pretty high heat, but fear not—this Venus sign is uniquely wired for it.

Audrey Hepburn represents the best of this Venus's courage, candor, and class. Audrey became a style icon, and it's no wonder: with feisty charisma, magnetism, and spunk, Venus in Aries gets noticed. Like Audrey, this Venus sign is noticeable, independent-minded, and tons of fun. An enthusiastic and adventuresome partner who can spar intelligently with her and respect her independent spirit has a good chance of creating the bond this Venus needs to make a relationship work. Love helps, too. But will this love be a sprint, or will it go the distance? The answer, as always, is up to her.

MAKING LOVE AND MISCHIEF

You're blessed with devastating magnetism, Venus in Aries. Some of the most hotly pursued people of all time share your Venus sign, including Marilyn Monroe, Elizabeth Taylor, and Jack Nicholson. Can you feel the hotness? Evolutionary astrologer Jeffrey Wolf Green has said that those born with Venus in Aries possess the strongest sex pheromones of all the Venus signs. This would be hard to validate and test scientifically, but Mars is the planetary ruler of Aries, and Mars is the planet of S-E-X. What do you get when you put one part sexy Mars with one part Venus, your own personal advertisement for relationships? A pheromone-fabulous cocktail called *you*.

You radiate a strong, passionate nature and gravitate toward people who are as self-oriented and committed to a life purpose as you. Once you lock on target with your ardent paramour and they lock on to you, the connection is instant and successful—at least initially. See, the lucky-in-love Aries knack brings with it the perpetual learning curve of Aries, too. This first sign of the zodiac arrives with the season of spring, so it embodies the youthful, impatient, and sometimes naive energy of springtime. After a long, hard, lonely winter, it's easy to rush into a connection with great sexual chemistry, but the hard part is sustaining the relationship past the initial rush of "oh boy, it's springtime!"

As is fitting for the first sign of the zodiac, you may experience firsts and false starts in relationships. Audrey Hepburn married several times, and Elizabeth Taylor married eight times. Venus in Aries needs to learn some precious lessons through her broken partnerships. She can be restless and impatient. In times of relationship stress, she may find it easy to focus her attention on herself instead of figuring out what her partner might need from her. This can lead to the demise of the relationship. Venus fire signs do need variety and excitement in their partnerships, and they will get that in one way or another, so channeling energy into a hobby she feels passionate about can alleviate Venus in Aries' insatiable restlessness. Starting her own business, exploring an art form, skydiving—activities like these provide a safe place for her adventuresome, passionate energy to burn.

Those with Venus in Aries may approach love dessert-first by diving right into a relationship that feels spectacular, but some discover that the best is saved for last. Audrey Hepburn called her last thirteen years, spent with Dutch actor Robert Wolders, the happiest time of her entire life. When asked by Barbara Walters about her rocky love life in an interview years before she died, Audrey (or her Venus) said, "It took me long enough." Don't worry, though. Chances are you won't have to wait that long, for you take an optimistic, hopeful approach to love. For the sign of perpetual springtime, there's always something to look forward to in love.

Venus in Aries might enjoy...

Starting projects, contact improv dance, metalworking, activities involving fire, competitive training and dancing, weightlifting, marathons, self-defense, rock 'n' roll, heavy metal, hot yoga, action movies, saunas, wearing red, fighting injustice, working up a sweat.

GIVE ME ADVENTURE AND EXCITEMENT

Mars, the energetic god of war, rules your Venus sign. When too much emotional drama rules the day, you may withdraw from a relationship altogether. Mars is also the god of physical stress and adrenaline rushes, which can work to your advantage by making things exciting, or to your disadvantage when relationship stress throws off your equilibrium. To be happy in love and life, you need plenty of other creative outlets, or you may seek adrenaline rushes by putting yourself in stressful interpersonal situations.

Action-loving and initiating, you need to be perpetually off and running in search of the next challenge. This doesn't have to be a new person, though it can be. Aries rules youth. For youthful Venus in Aries, it may be hard to distinguish physical lust from deeper affection or, eventually, love. About certain people you're instantly attracted to, you may eventually ask: was it love or just lust? Much can be answered by trying on different relationships for size and experimenting with your "type," which comes easily since this Venus sign is generally unafraid of interacting with new people. Hopefully the more relationship experience you gather, the more you will learn about what it takes to make a relationship work for you.

Those first steps into new love are always a rush, but to get along with someone for longer than a weekend rendezvous, or to take the relationship past the first blush of promise into full-blown love, Venus in Aries needs to see real potential for ongoing excitement and challenge in the relationship. To her paramours, this Venus sign promises much: courageous honesty, passion, the desire to push sexual and erotic boundaries, and a lifestyle of nonstop activity and excitement. She promises she will never, ever be boring. Can her partners make the same promise? They must, if she is to be happy. Venus in Aries' personal ad reads: "I am a thrill a minute. Expect nonstop action and laughs. Only like-minded need apply."

IN PRAISE OF PASSION

So you're in a relationship, and it's hot, fun, and sometimes difficult. Is all that conflict really necessary? If you're a Venus in Aries, you already know the answer. But for the rest of us, let's imagine being in a relationship where everything is peaceful all the time. Dinner is always served on time, and guess what? It's your favorite meal. You want to go out dancing at a club, and your partner agrees, staying out as late or coming home as early as you like. You're watching the game on television, and despite the fact that you're a fan of the away team, you root for the home team—because it's your partner's team. You talk about changing the kitty's litter box, and amazingly, there's no argument because you both agree that neither of you wants to do it. So you don't. The litter box piles up, but neither of you brings it up because that would only start a fight. Is this kind of peace good? We all know the answer to that question.

Peacefulness is worth striving for. We humans can be pretty horrible to each other when we're running around stressed out of our minds and high on adrenaline. But when keeping the peace becomes a way of avoiding the tough stuff in ourselves, our partner, and our relationship, it can be as destructive as a fight. This hardly makes Venus-in-Aries people battle-axes or warmongers. However, it does give these Venus born the ability to detect when there's not enough honesty in the relationship and when to do something about it. How? A battle cry is shouted! Sometimes this Venus sign will rush headlong into a battle over something small—say, over the litter box—when the real issue isn't being addressed. Deep down, Venus in Aries knows that conflict avoidance and complacency stymie everyone's growth.

Some Venus signs find that kind of peaceful predictability heavenly, but not Venus in Aries. Where there's no friction, no diversity of opinion, and no conflict, there's also no aliveness—and no spark. Venus in Aries thrives on sparks, if for no other reason than to keep passion and love alive.

Venus in Aries runs the risk of winning the battle but losing the war. This Venus is learning to pick her battles, but she is also learning that if she is to restore everyone to loving connection, she needs a winning strategy, a peaceful endpoint, and an "us" consciousness. In one of my favorite books, *If the Buddha Married*, psychotherapist Charlotte Kasl talks about fighting fair: "Remember, the point of conflict is not to be right or to discredit the other. It's to get to the other side so you can enjoy being together." Love is not a battle of me versus you. Venus in Aries needs to learn to address the right conflict, the better part of which is being honest with herself. That way she can avoid fulfilling the fortunetellers' dark prophecy for Venus in Aries: instead of having a passionate love affair with a person, her love affair is with drama, conflict, and her own restlessness. Casualties of the heart are avoidable.

Think with Your Venus Mantra, Venus in Aries

I am worthy and lovable just as I am. I openly share myself with everyone I meet. When I'm in touch with my creative passions, I can do anything. I can't control who does or does not love me, but I can choose healthy partners who love me for me. I am in charge of my love life.

Courageous and Confident

This Venus sign thrives on a level of risk. With her flip sense of humor, easy sense of destiny, and spunky confidence, Venus in Aries says, "I'm up for it!" She often projects an unshakably strong self-image, but her daredevil ways won't distract others from her vulnerable side, which shows up just as often.

Courage is a spiritual muscle for this Venus sign, growing stronger when regularly worked and flexed. Venus in Aries feels better about herself when she's taking a risk, stepping out on a ledge and doing the things she's always wanted to do, and these risks will scare her a little. Do you have a fear of performing in front of a live audience? Book a nightclub! Do you have a fear of exhibiting your art? Show a few friends. Do you need to have an honest discussion with your partner about your relationship? Sit down and have that talk today. Be honest and courageous and watch your relationships improve dramatically. That's how Venus in Aries acquires rock-solid confidence.

Courageously facing your fears also helps to keep your relationship life from becoming boring or, alternately, volatile. When your desire for excitement, risk-taking, and an honest expression of anger is unconscious or not expressed, all the power you possess can turn volatile or even dangerous. At best, you may attract fiery, risky, angry partners who simply reflect these traits to the degree that you don't express them. At worst, you can "attract" angry outbursts from others. A partner or loved one may turn abusive. In intimacy, you need to consciously step out of your comfort zone, or boredom may cause the embers of passion to cool.

Courageous energy is just energy, and it wants to be expressed one way or another. So for you Venus-in-Aries born who see yourselves as more of a wallflower than a warrior, start by speaking up, taking risks, being honest, and developing courage. No one is born with courage; we keep stepping out of our safe zone over and over, and courage builds into confidence. Guess what? That confidence will translate into more satisfying, empowering relationships with others.

HEART-SHY BUT GUTSY

We've all been hurt before. Especially after a few disappointing affairs, Venus-in-Aries people can find themselves a little gun-shy or commitment-phobic. (Remember that Phobos, or Fear, was the wartime frenemy of the war god Ares.) We may be afraid of getting hurt again. Or we may be reluctant to commit because when we're in a committed relationship, we're confronted with less attractive, unconscious attributes of our own character. If we have difficulty accepting and loving ourselves wholly, including our faults and flaws, we may shadow-box with our partners when we're actually fighting with our own shadow—the traits in ourselves that we misunderstand, devalue, judge, or are ashamed of. We may find it's easier to leave a relationship than to do patient, vulnerable open-heart surgery on ourselves.

It's humbling and courageous to be truly seen, and the courage to share all of it—ugly parts and all—is necessary for a Venus in Aries in love. It was Venus-in-Aries-born Marilyn Monroe who once said, "I'm selfish, impatient, and a little insecure. I make mistakes. I am out of control at times and hard to handle. But if you can't handle me at my worst, you sure as hell don't deserve me at my best." How's that for honesty? Venus in Aries, at her best, is emotionally forthright and honest about her difficult feelings. This Venus needs a partner who is equally candid, an emotionally courageous person.

Here's an exercise inspired by Marilyn: Take a deep breath and admit that you are, sometimes, hard to handle. You are not always on your best behavior. You are sometimes insecure, sometimes selfish, and sometimes down in the dumps. But you're also fun-loving, exciting to hang out with, and a sexual dynamo. By accepting yourself and then showing other people who you truly are, you will attract those who value your complex, fiery nature in total.

Confident and insecure, passionate and shy, gun-shy and gutsy—all of this is 100 percent you. If you can accept your whole self, you will attract people who find this interesting bag of contradictions absolutely lovable. As you become familiar with your flaws and frailties as well as your beauty—and still love yourself—you will attract a relationship with someone who can handle just about anything. Do so and you will be setting the foundation for true intimacy.

BEING ME WITH YOU

Aries is the sign of selfhood. Generally, Venus-in-Aries people are not averse to spending time alone, because they can always figure out how to entertain themselves.

As a Venus in Aries, you may actually be happier being alone for periods of time in order to recharge. Relationships can create a bit of stress for you, even those that are initially exciting. In relationships, you discover essential differences in taste, style, and ideology, and sometimes you find things in others that you don't like at all. Relationships tend to make you even more aware of your own individual preferences—the feelings, ideas, and desires that make you *you*. This is a beautiful thing, because for you, a relationship is a path to self-discovery and personal growth. But just as this process highlights differences and sparks precious self-awareness in you, opposing forces also create tension.

This isn't a reason to avoid relationships altogether. Our relationship with ourselves is the most important relationship we will ever have. Yet it is impossible to truly know ourselves without letting another person in. Our loved ones give us an angle on ourselves that is impossible to see otherwise. Your soulmates are helping you to learn the art of conflict resolution and teaching you the art of self-acceptance by loving you through the good, the bad, and the ugly. They are asking the same of you. Sure, love is hard sometimes and makes you angry. Sometimes it hurts and it's much easier to bolt than to put effort into the relationship—and *that's love, too*. Even in the best relationships, there are times when one or both partners question whether love is really enough, whether the restriction of freedom that committed love always entails is worth it. The trick is to keep opening yourself to love instead of shutting down. As you courageously open your heart to a soulmate, you earn something more valuable than gold to Aries: you learn how to be Me with You.

LOVE CHALLENGE

As a Venus in Aries, you may have a few lovers before finding the love of your life, or you may have more than one love of a lifetime—lucky you! No matter whether you consider them a soulmate or a time-of-life mate, all of your lovers have this in common: they will be passionate and purposeful, have a strong sense of self, face forward toward the future, be sexually vigorous, and be candid and possibly even visionary. Your lovers will become more evolved and sophisticated as you grow in self-awareness, because that's the reward for getting to know yourself better.

With your need for high-octane excitement, you enjoy partners who challenge you at a core level, and who may even push you to embody your creative strength and independence. Oh, you don't feel smart enough? Then a magna-cum-laude lover is perfect for you! You don't feel beautiful enough? Hello, Mr. GQ! Get the gist? You're in need of a partner who challenges you to step into your own light, provoking a bold act of outlandish self-love. Yours could be a power partnership. There are many examples of this: think about what Tommy Mottola did for Mariah Carey, or what Givenchy did for Audrey Hepburn. The best partners for you are those who value your creative power and candor and are confidence-building, not competitive. Mars (the ruler of Aries) is the planet of competition. With your Venus in Aries, you can attract partners who admire your strong sexuality and ambition but may also compete with you and fear your power. A relationship rife with power struggles is a telltale sign of this. If you're being undermined by a mate, ask yourself, *am I valuing myself enough?* This type of partner is here to teach you about your relationship to your self-worth, courage, and power.

YOUR EROTIC STRENGTH

Moxie. As a screen presence and style icon, Audrey Hepburn embodied the youthful, chic, and eternally sassy style of Aries. But it wasn't her signature look or what she wore that we admired most; it was her attitude, her lively spirit, that we fell in love with. The lady had moxie. You've got moxie. You have the gutsy backbone of famed classic movie stars. Guys, from a shamelessly stereotypical perspective, might even size you up as one "ballsy chick." Let's be honest: you intimidate and attract them. Moxie belongs to every self-made woman, and to possess moxie, one must also possess the know-how to make good things happen in life—which you do. It takes courage to move into the unknown, but courage looks so good on you! So when you're feeling blue, get your moxie on. Your pep, vigor, and spirited courage are contagious and moxify-ing. These are your erotic strengths.

IF YOU'RE IN LOVE WITH VENUS IN ARIES...

Your Venus-in-Aries partner wants a relationship with someone who challenges her to boldly take the necessary risks that make love and life thrilling. There are two types of Venus in Aries: the shrinking violet and the daredevil. The former makes you drag her to the public-speaking class, workshop, or skydiving lesson, but once there, she blows you away with her gutsiness. The latter is an impulsive risk-taker. With either type, expect an edgy, exciting relationship. Venus in Aries craves emotional candor and will ask you to be an open book with her.

Venus in Aries is classically compatible with fire signs (Aries, Leo, Sagittarius) and air signs (Gemini, Libra, Aquarius). Taurus and Scorpio are clever matches, too—two equally strong-willed and steadfast signs that help Aries to stand up for herself while fostering a deep, abiding, supportive connection.

Venus in Taurus

♉

They say it is better to be poor and happy than rich and miserable, but how about a compromise like moderately rich and just moody?

~PRINCESS DIANA, VENUS IN TAURUS

YOUR LOVE ELEMENT

Peaceful, sensible, sensual Earth is surely a planet floating around in the Milky Way, but unlike that faraway feeling of looking through a telescope, there's nothing esoteric or out-there about the element of earth; earth is hands-on and right here. Oh, the joy of earthworms! The pleasure of watching the life cycle of butterflies! Ode to the ladybug! The mating of mammals! The natural world inspires all of creation toward procreation. We find peaceful ease and connection in Mother Nature, too, as earth encourages us to relax into her bounty of goodness, to appreciate and enjoy what can be seen, felt, tasted, and touched by all of the senses. Heaven can be a place on Earth, a Garden of Eden designed for relaxation and pleasure.

Your Secret Desire

Like the words in that old Coca-Cola commercial, "I'd like to teach the world to sing in perfect harmony…," you live to create a harmony of the senses through music, good food, lovemaking, and laughter. Born with both feet planted on terra firma, you know the secret to creating harmony is to relax, enjoy, and appreciate our time on Earth, with each other. There are a million ways to do this, including planting a garden, singing a song, and making love. A bear hug at the right moment will do the trick, too.

Your Love Charms

- Your salt-of-the-earth bodaciousness. Whether you're dressed to the nines for a social event or casually hanging ten, you always keep it real. Even when glammed out, you give off a sensual and down-to-earth vibe.

- People trust you because you are, as the French say, *bien dans ta peau*—comfortable in your own skin. This at-ease body sense gives you a clear talent for putting those in your company completely, instantly, and utterly at ease.

- You trust your body instincts. Whether you're making a decision or talking your way out of a jam, if you feel calm and relaxed, you know it's the right thing to do. You can always trust your body's wisdom to guide you in your next move.

- Your fierce loyalty and devotion to the ones you love. You can be tough about what you want, and as fierce as a bull. But with a tender lover, you're as cuddly and huggable as a bunny.

- You're a paradoxical earth mama with Hollywood starlet appeal. People are intrigued by your commonsense nature, champagne good taste, and sensual presence.

- The more you value your innate talent and strengths, the more your value increases in the world. You can make a very good thing into an even better one.

- Your spiritual understanding of and connection to all of nature. Whether you're a medicine woman, massage therapist, animal lover, or health food enthusiast, both your talents and your income can be found in earthly realms. You gain spiritual congruence with the physical world by forming values around the people and things that are most important to you.

YOUR LOVE GODDESS

Jane Russell (1921–2011) used her small-town-gal assets to become a pin-up queen. In her time, Jane Russell was the brunette Marilyn Monroe; to Marilyn's movie *Gentlemen Prefer Blondes*, Jane responded with *Gentlemen Marry Brunettes*. Touché! There wasn't a more wholesome pin-up girl than Jane Russell. Jane experienced sexism and hardship, such as several rape attempts and an abortion that left her unable to conceive; yet she was hardy, resilient, and resolute in the face of obstacles—all Taurus traits you possess.

There was more to Jane's beauty than meets the eye; her body of work did a lot for the advancement of women. An original ringleader of the erotic muses of Hollywood—women celebrated for their great beauty and glamour—Jane was one of the first women whose name in show business became synonymous with an uncommonly busty, full-figured beauty. Jane brought glamour to robust beauty. In her time, Jane generated newfound enthusiasm in the general public for the curvy womanly figure; yes, Jane, real women do have curves.

Jane demonstrated the art of being relaxed and comfortable in your body no matter your shape or size. How you feel about your body will always be tied to whether you move through life with bold confidence or feelings of inadequacy. As a Venus in Taurus, you rely on that strong, clear connection to your body, as your ease in your own skin is what draws others toward you. Always remember that no matter your shape or size, Venus in Taurus possesses a sensuality that drives mortal men and women wild.

You may not see how your body image and self-worth so intimately intertwine, but Jane's life demonstrates how the two work together. Jane demonstrated that body ease has substantial value, and without the confidence to take herself seriously, she likely would never have resourcefully plumbed her own talent, turning her physical assets into bankable ones. Many Venus-in-Taurus born have to overcome doubt about their physical beauty and self-worth. Jane stubbornly insisted on sharing her Goddess-given assets with the world, and for her guts and class she earned the description "mean, moody, and magnificent."

Beauty and talent come in all forms. We can have a beautiful singing voice, make gorgeous jewelry, or be a goddess to partners and friends. Yet one thing tends to be true: to claim our creative gifts in the world and be loved, we need to be secure at a basic level. We need to be at peace in and with our bodies. We need healthy self-esteem. When you love yourself and your body, there's a greater chance you'll take your gifts and skills—your talents—seriously.

Venus in Taurus is notoriously money- and security-conscious. You do enjoy all the pleasures money can buy, but "having enough" symbolizes something deeper for you: it gives you peace of mind and the security to relax. And the more at ease you feel in your skin, the more worthy and capable you tend to feel, and the more likely you will be to take a risk on your own talents. By trusting that you are enough, you gravitate toward bankrolling your natural assets. You also share your creative gifts—one of the highest forms of Venus work in this world.

BODY EASE

Venus loves being in her own home sign of Taurus, meaning that all other things being equal, she is exceedingly comfortable, relaxed, and at home in her own skin. Cultivating a calm, easygoing lifestyle, with plenty of sensory diversions as well as interactions with nature and animals, is vital to keeping that peaceful, easy feeling on tap. Imagine the weight and feel of the smooth, white marble statue of Venus de Milo, a timeless icon of Venus. Look to her for a reflection of your own relaxed, self-possessed confidence and slightly modest nature.

Having your Venus in her home sign of Taurus means you are a true daughter of the goddess Aphrodite, in her earthy aspect. Blessed with an appetite for good food, laughter, and pleasures of the senses, Aphrodite is at her most delightful in Taurus, where she indulges her decadent tastes for food, wine, and lovemaking. She loves to relax and enjoy life, and although she is by no means materialistic, this Venus sign thoroughly adores the creature comforts that money can buy. These are the ways that Venus relaxes herself and puts others at ease.

Ideally, every Venus in Taurus would be comfortable in her own body. After all, you were born with a sensual animal magnetism that other Venus signs covet. However, for Venus-in-Taurus women of today, body ease has gone all orange and red alert. No woman is exempt from the pressure to conform to a standard of beauty that dichotomizes the spirit and the flesh. Body and beauty ideals seem to change with the wind. Whereas Botticelli's Venus (with enough belly for a muffin top) was once the standard of beauty, that is no longer the case. Today, it's Kate "nothing tastes as good as skinny feels" Moss. That's wonderful for Kate, but her brand of beauty wouldn't have been so popular centuries (or even decades) ago.

Even if we know that all body types are beautiful, consumerism manipulates us, preying on our deepest insecurities. Insecurity is the great marketing device. Aphrodite/Venus is the mistress of using illusion and artifice to her best advantage. And why not? Cosmetic surgery, great jeans, and amazing shoes can do wonders for a woman's figure and body confidence. However, it's also true that even the most physically gorgeous woman can be missing the inner magical quality we readily recognize in truly radiant and beautiful women. This kind of inner beauty trumps all.

So what is true beauty, anyway? Beauty is a way of being in the world. It's also not just one thing. True beauty, like happiness, has many components: a healthy body, an intellectually stimulated mind, emotional well-being, spiritual peace—all together, these create ease in one's own skin. Those who are born with Venus in Taurus need to be comfortable in their own skin. This concept is tied not only to body confidence, but also to how we live and with whom we associate. If we are in the right place (an environment that is compatible with our nature) and with the right people (those who notice and honor our desires and appreciate what we have to offer), we will be comfortable and at ease in the other areas of our lives. Having body confidence, feeling connected to the natural environment, and being with peaceful, easygoing people all put Venus in Taurus at ease.

Venus in Taurus might enjoy...

Cooking, eating, massage, lounging, chocolate, body-work, ceramics, sculpting, modeling, gardening, taking it easy, nature, animals, the smell of baking bread or rising dough (as in money), creating any art form with your own hands.

LOVE YOUR ANIMAL

Body politics aside, there's an easy way to support and uplift this Venus sign. Taurus is the sign of animals and ease. Animals don't judge their habits, appetites, bodies, and procreative drives; humans do. Being in the presence of a Venus-in-Taurus person who has a good relationship to her body and sensual appetite is like being in the easy presence of your favorite animal. We become more grounded, present, and accepting. We instantly relax. We open to love.

Venus in Taurus needs to embrace her inner animal, that unique creature who has the cravings, sensual yearnings, desires, and habits of any animal. Ask yourself: *If I were an animal, what would I be? What does the animal in me want? Do I see our animal appetites—the sensual and sexual drives we all have—as healthy or bad? Why?* Your happiness depends on embracing your animal desires, and on whether you judge your preferences as bad or good.

If loving and honoring her animal nature puts this Venus at ease, there's no quicker way to make her unhappy than to take her out of her element. Just as polar bears love the Arctic cold but could be harmed or even die in the dry, scorching-hot

Sahara desert, when Venus-in-Taurus born are in the right environment, with the right people, they thrive. The right environment has economic security and the guaranteed love of friends and family. When this Venus feels at home, at ease, and comfortable with her environment, peace, love, and happiness flow quite organically from that place.

There's another reason why Venus in Taurus needs to know what the inner animal wants—when we don't, we can sabotage our best efforts. In an attempt to comfort or ground herself, this Venus has been known to use food or shopping as a crutch, to quell loneliness or other bodily appetites and desires. What woman hasn't used a pint of ice cream or a pair of shoes as a substitute for a therapist, a phone call to a girlfriend, or sex? Sometimes it's okay to eat ice cream; other times it helps to understand what's really going on.

With your Venus in Taurus, you benefit from time spent outdoors in nature and with four-legged creatures. The natural world has immediate benefits; being outdoors, gardening, farming, and raising animals all help you relax, unwind, and center. You may find frequent nature breaks balancing and essential to your happiness. It's fun to compare human nature to animals, too, as there are many funny parallels between the two. Any Taurus planet could spend hours watching the Discovery Channel or Animal Planet—it is a sign that learns so much about human behavior from animals! Likewise, animals are inexplicably drawn to this Venus's gentle presence. Your spirit animal may be an owl, a rabbit, a bird, or a tiger, but you have a special affinity with the bull or cow, sacred to the sign of Taurus.

THINK WITH YOUR VENUS MANTRA, VENUS IN TAURUS

I am the living, breathing embodiment of the Earth Goddess, and I have a bootyliscious bod to boot. I am physically sensual, creatively gifted, and resourceful with my talents. As I trust in my natural Goddess-given gifts and share them with the world, my gifts appreciate and are appreciated.

SEXUAL AND SENSUAL

Modern sexual relationships move faster than a bullet train, at least in the United States. An appreciative glance on the subway can lead to a sexual invitation faster than you can sweetly demure, "No, thank you." This fast and easy approach to sex leaves no room for going slow, for taking time to get to know and trust each other and relax, which is what Venus in Taurus needs most.

Yet, this Venus's grounded body centeredness, ability to establish an easy rapport, and earthy sensuality are so exciting to the trigger-happy Adams of the world that they are quick to act on what they see. Venus in Taurus possesses the biblical beauty of Eve and carries her tempting, forbidden apple. This has undoubtedly put her in more than a few interesting situations with the opposite sex!

Venus isn't sex—though she loves sex and can be sexy like no other. "Venus," says astrologer Dana Gerhardt, "is the girl at the ticket booth, representing your preferred entrance into eroticism." This Venus prefers to take her time. Because the sensuality before the sex requires us to slow down, Venus in Taurus is the mistress of foreplay. Every woman knows foreplay is one of the best parts of sex! To enjoy foreplay, let alone sex, we need to slow down and be present. We need to relax and tune in to our bodies. To be pleasured by her lover, a woman with Venus in Taurus need only slow down, listen to her body, and let her inner animal out.

It's all too easy to move things along sexually in a relationship, though generally, with your Venus in Taurus, you prefer the slow train to pleasure, taking time to linger and to allow someone not just to tell you but to *show* you who they are. You are attracted to purposeful, steady types who do what they say and say what they mean, and discovering this takes time. People with too much flash and bling are a turn-off; you are turned on by salt-of-the-earth types. If you're getting mixed messages about a person's intentions, you can accurately evaluate the person's character just by how you feel in your body when you're around them.

This Venus's secret is that she listens to her body with all her senses and always honors her own instincts. Venus in Taurus takes the time to pay attention to the sensations of touch, intuition, feeling, smell, and taste, because they are a form of Venus intelligence. She pays attention to her inner animal, noticing what satisfies her and what leaves her hungry or wanting. But this isn't the wild animal of, say, Aries. The seduction of adventuresome Venus in Aries is radically different from that of gentle Venus in Taurus, who reveals herself slowly over time.

This Venus is a true Eve—there is no need to be modest about it, though you may be. Your modesty endears you to others, making them trust you. Your modesty, like the half-revealed Venus de Milo, is also an erotic gesture, an invitation to feast on the pleasures of the senses. As you awaken to the spine-tingling effect you have on both sexes, your Taurean "mean, moody, and magnificent" streak may kick in, and with it, the confidence to honor yourself by unapologetically asking for what you desire most. When this happens, the Goddess has arrived.

NATURAL ASSETS

Taurus rules money, and Venus in Taurus loves the security that money provides even more than the opportunity for decadence and sensual indulgence (though this Venus loves that, too). Security and stability relax her. Fortunately, she tends to magnetize abundance, often through her own resourcefulness.

Even though she has a penchant for pampering, this Venus doesn't need a crate of Beluga caviar and Donald Trump's bank account to make her happy. This is often a very down-to-earth Venus sign for whom simple pleasures can bring the greatest delights. The Venus-in-Taurus women I've known bear this out with their love for tea, herbs, aromatherapy, nature walks, and gardening. Sensual gifts, luxury, and art can certainly bring them pleasure, but giving to others, mothering, spending time with animals, or working with the earth are more satisfying.

The Venus-in-Taurus path to happiness isn't "out there" or confusing; it's practical and grounded and only involves working with what you already have. Sometimes it's literally working with the earth or working with your hands; other times this means going into business for yourself or with your partner, and applying the talents that come naturally to you in ways that make money so you can take more spa days and buy more creature comforts. For some Venus-in-Taurus born, this means taking a good look at the world around them and making it better; they clean up Mother Earth and take care of kids, kin, and animals.

This applies to material life, too. Financial insecurity can plague this Venus sign, but earthy Venus in Taurus is exceedingly resourceful and practical and knows the true value of a thing when she sees it. This Venus will beautify an old house, hold on to valuable family heirlooms, or carry on an ancestral gift or legacy simply because it makes sense to do so. With your Venus in this sign, your penchant for pampering, your artistic gifts, and your resourcefulness can make you money as sure as the sky is blue. When you polish up what you have, when you offer your natural gifts to the world, when you decide to do what you love and earn hard cash for it, you will know: everything you could ever need, you already have in your possession.

STABILITY AT ALL COSTS

Self-possessed and self-reliant, Venus in Taurus is learning to trust in her ability to move through the world and her relationships, guided by her inner sense of values. This is how she aligns with her partners, too. Whether the subject is politics of food, body, or government, this Venus sign gravitates toward those people who reflect her preferences and feelings exactly. She can embrace people from all walks of life, but just as a polar bear wouldn't mate with a giraffe, she is only intimately comfortable with her same species, more so than any other Venus sign. When she finds someone whose values mirror hers, she's made a dear friend for life.

Comfort, likeness, and agreement among the same species can hinder growth, though. Occasionally a Venus in Taurus will wake up one day to find the only thing her relationship has helped her grow is the mold on the expired carton of yogurt in her refrigerator. At that point she may realize she's sacrificed growth for stability, and the risks and rewards of a passionate, unpredictable love affair for security. When that happens, this Venus sign yearns for greener pastures, but that doesn't mean she will seek them! Venus in Taurus's ability to inwardly comfort herself gives her the ability to stay in relationships that have long outlived their purpose. Her self-reliance and self-possession enable her to stay with partners others may find predictable or even boring. Instead of getting her growth needs met through the relationship, she values the stability it brings her and cultivates hobbies and friendships; she cooks, eats, and travels. She enjoys other areas of life with gusto.

For a Venus in Taurus, the partnership must be a monogamous one, whether the relationship is lifelong or short-term. Partners who engage in sexual indiscretions or are too loose with their erotic and sexual boundaries—even if it's "just flirting"—erode her confidence in subtle or overt ways. Insecurity can plague this Venus sign, leading her to engage in the ugly habit of comparing herself to others in terms of body, status, and self-image.

Erotically, Venus in Taurus wants to belong to someone, to possess and be possessed. There's nothing more satisfying for Venus in Taurus than belonging to someone and all that implies—cooking together, sharing kids and pets, etc. She needs the physical solidity and material abundance of terra firma from her partnership. She wants to be the sensual centerpiece in her partner's eyes. She wants to be needed by her lover, to feed her lover with food and sex, and to grow old together.

SAFE AND SECURE

Being well aware of the danger of throwing your pearls to swine, you approach relationships more cautiously than some other Venus signs. This makes you more inclined not to share your heart and body until the person has earned your trust, and not until you're ready. You aren't afraid to commit; on the contrary, you are steadfast and true. Potential mates quickly learn that there's no monkeying around with you. When you get serious about someone, you mean business.

Well, mostly. There are exceptions to every Venus standard. For instance, fiery individuals (those with Mars, Aries, or fire signs prominent in their birth charts) will be more inclined to throw caution to the wind and jump into relationships quickly, before establishing a level of trust. Aspects to Venus from other planets (like Jupiter, Pluto, or Uranus) can modify the expression of any Venus. When other, louder planets are involved, Venus in Taurus's natural inclination to take it easy may fly out the window.

If you have Venus in Taurus but are basically all over the place when it comes to dating and partnering, you might try taking it slow for a change. You might try letting the other person earn your trust before you give them your body. A simple Venus-sign strategy can bring great success in love where your other relationship strategies have failed. For instance, you might try sizing up a potential partner by checking in with your body to gauge how safe and secure you feel with the person. If you get a "yes," move forward no more than one space. Then, a few days later, check in again. Venus's methods work reliably.

Astrology texts say that Venus in Taurus favors simplicity and comfort over psychological complexity and growth in relationships. That's because Taurus is opposite the emotionally and psychologically complex sign of Scorpio. Your love strategy is to take people at face value, to believe what you can see, taste, touch, and feel. Nothing is wrong with this—until you meet a deceptive snake charmer. Once bitten, twice shy. Over time, you learn to trust your body and senses to tell you what you need to know about another. Learn to listen to this earthy instinct. It won't lead you astray. Likewise, if, in your desire for the easy life, you turn on the television, go on a spending spree, or decide not to have a difficult conversation because it would cause you or your partner discomfort, then recognize that conflict and insecurity can motivate growth—which is good for every relationship. Safety and permanence in this life are fleeting, anyhow.

Your natural soulmates are easygoing folks who give you a sense of security and safety. They appreciate your strengths and relish your sensual and easy approach to love and pleasure. They are easy to be around; they simply make you feel good about yourself. It may sound old-fashioned, but your soulmate may even be a partner who demonstrates a good work ethic and is able to make money, which could be a big turn-on for you. You're learning to value your own gifts, so a partner who makes tangible efforts in the world inspires you to make it happen for yourself. They support you in making the most of your natural assets. They see you as the goddess you are.

YOUR EROTIC STRENGTH

Presence. There's no ulterior motive with you, no psychological complexity to unravel, no secrets, no hidden agendas. Psychologically complex folks will be drawn to your presence simply because you calm them down. For some of us, being with you is like sitting next to a mountain stream on a clear day. Your Zen-like demeanor puts us at peace. While the rest of the world is trying to unravel their confusion, you are the rock in the harbor, the one we come to for healing and unconditional love. What a gift you are to the rest of us! You often marvel at how unnecessarily and ridiculously complex we human beings make things. Sigh. By offering a pot of tea and a smile to your loved ones, you encourage us to stop and smell the roses. And because you're there, we do.

IF YOU'RE IN LOVE WITH VENUS IN TAURUS...

Your Venus in Taurus craves a straightforward, easygoing love affair with someone equally straightforward and reliable. She's a consummate lover who aims to please, so you'll never have to guess where you stand with her. She is as peace-loving as she is strong-willed and stubborn about what she wants. A good meal, bottle of wine, and luxurious massage will send her over the top.

Venus in Taurus is classically compatible with earth signs (Taurus, Virgo, Capricorn) and water signs (Cancer, Scorpio, Pisces), though a fun-loving and equally loyal Leo could be the cat's meow for this Venus. Leo loves to provide materially for their lion's pride, but both Venus signs will need to learn to yield the floor to the other instead of vying for world domination.

Venus in Gemini

Ⅱ

I love you more than my own skin
and even though you don't love me the same way,
you love me anyways, don't you?
And if you don't, I'll always have the hope that you do,
and I'm satisfied with that.
Love me a little. I adore you.

~FRIDA KAHLO, VENUS IN GEMINI

YOUR LOVE ELEMENT

All-knowing, indefinable, fresh air is the spiritual presence of life. Air constantly and invisibly moves and travels vast distances in a single whoosh. News travels from one place to another, conversations are carried great distances on the wind—nothing is hidden from air's curiosity. With every word uttered and every road traveled, air is our faithful companion, carrying messages, passing secrets from one point to the next, and listening, forever and always in motion. Air needs plenty of freedom to move and to change—traveling back and forth, connecting one to the other, moving through, around, betwixt, and in between, and hungrily exploring new people, ideas, and places. This element dislikes being pinned down, but it can be harnessed. If you've ever flown a kite, you've harnessed the power of air, but that's only because air loves a moving adventure. As long as it's kept moving, air is happy, as trapped air grows as stale and boring as yesterday's news.

YOUR SECRET DESIRE

To use your DNA to clone your other half, your twin flame. But wait, you've already done that! So now all you have to do is find that person. You joyfully take up the journey, getting into all sorts of interesting and tricky situations along the way. No matter where you are or who you're with, if your curiosity is piqued and your mind is engaged, you're game.

YOUR LOVE CHARMS

- A mercurial ability to change it up at whim. You know dress-up isn't just for kids; when we change our clothing, style, or minds, we feel alive and brand-new. That's the fresh, youthful, effervescent quality of Gemini.

- Living in the ever-changing, dynamic moment. In the moment, you improvise. You make it up as you go along. It's all happening already in a stream-of-consciousness kind of way, and you're at your best living in the now.

- Your love advertisement reads: "Open to new experiences." It's a good thing. Chances are you need to have several significant and varied relationships in your lifetime.

- Your ingenious ability to finesse your way into anyone's heart. You've got the mad skills of Cleopatra, who wrapped herself in a Persian carpet and tumbled out when Caesar unrolled it. Caesar was so charmed by her ingenuity that she became his mistress.

- Your adaptability and fluidity. Your clear ability to meet people where they're at gives you a universal sex appeal, making you sensually appealing to both genders.

- You've got your finger on the pulse of what's happening right now. Like a beat poet or beat reporter, when you're tuned in, you're also turned on, and your running commentary on what's happening makes you interesting to others.

- Your smarts. You appreciate someone with a quick wit and a lively, inquiring mind, because you have that, too. Intelligence is a big turn-on for you.

YOUR LOVE GODDESS

The life story of Frida Kahlo (1907–1954), the Mexican artist, was tragic and inspiring. Frida's face is now universally known in all corners of the world for the remarkable way she communicated grace through suffering, for the beauty, pain, and hope in her art. But to those who knew her, Frida was two people: Frida no. 1 was goddess-like, resilient, and the epitome of feminine strength, while Frida no. 2 drank, swore like a man, and was often tough and crude. As complex as she was artistically prolific, Frida embodied the duality and ingenuity of the sign of the Twins, a sign allied with self-expression, and a sign that moves easily between two worlds.

There's a family photo that features Frida at a tender young age. Among her sisters, mother, father, and relatives, Frida stands out, and not just because she is so striking. What is most captivating is her daring: she is the only girl not wearing a dress. Frida boldly wore a man's suit. This may seem inconsequential today, but the photo was taken at the turn of the twentieth century. Like Frida, those born with Venus in Gemini are curious, irreverent, and sometimes provocative. Often bold and fearlessly experimental, this Venus loves to push boundaries.

Frida was constantly crossing boundaries—of race, culture, artistic convention, political ideology, and sexuality. Frida's bisexuality was an open secret. She had multiple affairs with the unconventional thinkers and artists of her time. Truly open to all walks of life, Venus in Gemini learns to diversify her interests, and new connections open her to new relationships. Open-minded, experimental, and curious, she often has universal sex appeal. While bisexuality may be a choice for Venus in Gemini, this Venus sign isn't more likely to be bisexual than any other. However, Venus in Gemini is experimental and does need to try on different relationships for size and fit. Gemini is the sign of youth and learning. This Venus sign enjoys learning from love. Ideally she will gather some experience in love before settling down and committing to a lifelong relationship. Otherwise she may find herself bored or chronically torn, ambivalent in love.

Courting a Venus in Gemini is like attempting to catch a lightning bug: fun, entertaining, never a dull moment…and you just never know what will happen next. This Venus sign is attracted to people who pique her intellectual curiosity, who indulge her experimental side and love of stimulating conversation. Her effect on other people is like a breath of fresh air—effervescent and refreshing. There is an innate restlessness driving her, but as Venus in Gemini courts new experiences, she keeps cracking the riddle of her own heart, at least until the next one appears. Gemini's unquenchable desire for new experiences ensures that she'll never run out of questions. Once she's chosen you as her life mate, you may be as perplexed and delighted by her as she is by herself, but you won't be bored.

Venus in Gemini loves to cross-pollinate ideas, experiences, and people, a divine form of play for her. While Frida had many love interests, her twin flame, husband Diego Rivera, was an artist and independent thinker like herself. Unfortunately, Frida and Diego are as famous for their unhappiness as their art, but I challenge that conclusion and hope you will, too. I'm not quick to sell their romance as an unhappy one; from what we know about their relationship through letters and firsthand accounts, it was passionate and jealous, painful and beautiful, tender and loving. We may not know how Frida ultimately felt about their relationship, but for Venus in Gemini there are no failures in love, only experiences and learning. Frida and Diego were exceptional in all regards. Their marriage, and their love affairs outside of it, certainly challenged the container of their union and almost broke it, but they were committed. They showed their commitment to learning about intimacy in a way that many of us do—by marrying each other. Twice.

TWO HAPPY

Gemini is the sign of questions and confusion—of this, or that? It's not as scary as it sounds! When we're confused, we're not so certain about our perceptions, and therefore we're open to new possibilities and insights we might not have otherwise had. Without self-questioning, we get stuck in ruts of habit, which is anathema to Gemini.

To avoid getting stuck again and to keep growing, Venus in Gemini enjoys exploration, wonder, and questioning. To avoid ruts, she loves frequent changes of scenery—day trips are great for this Venus. Her interests keep changing, too. First, it was tai chi: she fell in love with the fluid movement and the way it made her feel so relaxed and centered. Then one day at the bookstore she discovered a new Tarot deck, which rocked her spiritual world. Then, when a friend introduced her to ancient runes, she heard the voice of her Celtic ancestors speaking so clearly and plainly that she signed up for a class immediately. Venus in Gemini loves to learn. She surveys rather than specializes. She cross-pollinates, taking a little of this and adding this to that. She may not need to choose one idea, person, or interest over the others—she will find a way to have it all.

Every astrology book will tell you that Venus in Gemini needs plenty of freedom. From a karmic perspective, in the past, Venus-in-Gemini born likely were stuck in relationships that didn't leave much room for growth, wonder, and new experiences. As a result, they need to gather more relationship experience, which may lead to multiple significant relationships.

This is the Venus sign that needs to play the field for a while—the perpetual bachelorette by her own design. Venus in Gemini has an underlying need to learn about relationships, and the only way to learn is through experience. So think twice the next time you yank the chain of your flirtatious, uncommitted Venus-in-Gemini friend—don't be so quick to judge her behavior.

Gemini is all about learning from experience, and this Venus often needs more than one partner to do that. Yet Venus in Gemini can perpetually circle the appetizer table and never actually reach the main course: intimacy. The true fruit of a love relationship, intimacy, can't be acquired in a weekend workshop, because unlike falling in love with a new subject, when we fall in love with someone, we need to specialize in the subject: us. This requires a feet-first, all-hands-on-deck commitment. Granted, the person you choose to give your energy, affection, and time to will likely have a few qualities and behaviors you'd probably rather cash your cards in on than tolerate, but that's no reason to call the whole relationship off (and confirm the opinions of a host of astrologers who insist on calling yours a "fickle" Venus sign).

Eventually, Venus in Gemini must be willing to trade some freedom for the stability of committed love. This Venus can and does enjoy committed love. People with this Venus sign are open-minded, smart, and stimulating partners, and the love they offer others is the excitement of growing, exploring, talking, and learning together. They want to push the envelope and be provocative. They want to talk about anything and everything. Naturally their ideal mate is not sitting on the couch watching life happen on the sidelines—this quickly leads to the Gemini malaise: boredom. Their twin flame is a dynamic person who lives life fully engaged.

Venus in Gemini might enjoy...

Travel, talking, writing, learning, trying new things, playing dress-up, open minds, studying languages, reading, dancing, listening to your senses, touch and massage therapy, experimenting with different tastes and styles of music, being provocative.

CONVERSANT AND CURIOUS

Frankly, my darling, you're a natural flirt. You know how to start a conversation with just about anyone. While some folks avoid casual conversation, you believe in striking up a conversation just to see where it leads. Each new person you meet brings something new to the mix, and when you're moving from person to person and interest to interest, you're turned on and tuned in. We see that elfin twinkle in your eye, which you know we find so irresistibly charming.

To be a great conversationalist, you've got to be a great listener. As the adage goes, God gave you two ears and one mouth for a reason, and this is an appropriate motto for Gemini. Gemini moves quickly through the world, so taking the time to really listen and connect is paramount. For some Venus in Gemini, the thing they must do is the hardest: stop gathering information, bouncing around, and cross-pollinating, and instead just listen.

In relationships, listening—really listening—is the best love therapy a Venus in Gemini could ask for. You love diversity in people and interests for a reason: there's value in hearing diverse points of view so very different from your own. Also, when we consider other people's points of view, our minds and spirits are stretched to new limits. We practice empathy; we begin to really understand another. What we don't want to do is get stuck on hearing only one voice—ours.

In a long-term relationship, it's easy to start to tune out. We hear our partner's favorite story, the one they love to tell, over and over again. Or we know them so well that we can anticipate their thoughts and finish their sentences. When we tune out, we lose touch with the magic of the present moment, which leads to boredom. To keep love fresh, this Venus needs to live in the present moment, where nothing is predictable and anything could happen. The present moment is always an exciting place to be, full of new curiosities to discover about your lover, new interests to pursue, and new conversations to have. So next time you find yourself getting bored, listen up. Bring a breath of fresh air to your partnership by dropping the storyline and really tuning in.

SHOULD I STAY OR SHOULD I GO?

Over and over this Venus wonders: is this "the one" or not? Venus in Gemini is constantly having this type of conversation with herself, and when the questions pile up, she ends up in a quagmire of ambivalence. Ambivalence is feeling divided about how you feel about a person, idea, or relationship. Venus in Gemini says, *You think* you're *going crazy? Try being me.* Ambivalence is maddening for all. Even if we're committed, our feelings of ambivalence can drain the romance and joy right out of our partnerships.

If we're ambivalent, at some point we will likely collapse in exhausted confusion. Maybe we're just tired of all the self-questioning. Maybe we break up. Without conducting elaborate surveys, it would be hard for us astrologers to know whether this Venus sign (which favors multiples) is likelier than others to get divorced or have multiple marriages; however, we do know that for the Venus who prizes learning, there is no such thing as a failed relationship—it's all learning; it's all experience.

Truly none of us ever know if we'll wake up one morning to discover that we no longer love the person we thought we did. No one can give us that certainty. That's no reason to avoid committed intimacy, though—to perpetually circle the appetizer course at the buffet of life without ever risking your heart on another. While gathering experience is the right thing to do for a time, a committed relationship offers intimacy with ourselves that nothing else does, and that leads to profound learning.

Not knowing how a relationship will turn out is part of the exciting journey for this Venus sign. You may not know if your partner is entirely right for you or how long you'll be together, but if you're having fun today studying the secret lives of bees and monkeying around, you're on the right track. You can have a deep conversation about Sartre or the validity of astrology tonight, and a profound case of the giggles tomorrow. You, above all Venus signs, can enjoy the beauty of not knowing.

THINK WITH YOUR VENUS MANTRA, VENUS IN GEMINI

I know my twin soul exists, and I'll have fun looking and playing. I was born to get into all kinds of playfully precarious situations in love and have a blast learning from them. My stunt double is doing the same. When we meet, we'll have tons to share and talk about. In fact, we probably won't shut up.

FOOTLOOSE AND FREE

I have a Venus-in-Gemini friend who loves to dance. Her partner likes to dance, but not the same style, so she goes to her dance club with another male friend. She's got Venus in Gemini—she needs two dance partners to be happy! It's perfectly sane to acknowledge that our mate can't possibly fulfill all our needs. This Venus sign enjoys shaking up the system, stepping outside the agreed-upon roles in her relationship, and trying on new ways of being together for a time.

The Twins need to regularly stretch beyond what they see around them. Take a weekend trip. Attend a talk or lecture. Venus in Gemini also loves being absorbed in the pleasurable activity of the present moment, together with another fun twin soul. So cook dinner together, and instead of playing a solo, make beautiful music together. Love the one you're with and be here now.

This Venus is happiest footloose and fancy-free. Ideally the partner of a Venus-in-Gemini person accepts and appreciates her need for a wide social circle and possibly many different types of relationships, some of which may not be mainstream. Likewise, this Venus won't take kindly to possessive, controlling, or chronically jealous partners. Venus in Gemini needs breathing space. Partners who are jealous of her time, fickle about her friends, or inconsolable about her companions will really cramp this Venus sign's style. While jealousy is a healthy human emotion expressing how deeply and lovingly attached we are to our mate, and is present in every intimate love relationship because we care so deeply, possessiveness of another person's freedom, friends, and time is not healthy. A strong couple can work through healthy jealousy in one or both partners, but a chronically jealous person is incredibly difficult for this Venus sign to handle. Venus in Gemini is extremely sensitive to having her freedom encroached upon.

KEEP ON MOVING

William Shakespeare, a Venus in Gemini, wrote, "Pleasure and action make the hours seem short." Oh, how time flies when you're on the go and having fun! When you're feeling lifeless, stuck, or blue, movement and conversation, learning and socializing, creating art, and dancing are all good for you.

You relax in a way many people don't: by being mentally and/or physically busy. A steady diet of information is your aphrodisiac, so intelligent conversation in the form of a romantic poem or passionate e-mail exchange is a favorite form of foreplay for you. When you feel stuck and disengaged, learn something new. Grow; go somewhere—anywhere at all. Let your interests run wild and amok.

Venus in Gemini requires stimulation, growth, and learning from all of her partnerships, especially her numero uno. A banker who only reads the stock market numbers may not be the one for her, but a banker who reads Sanskrit and is going trekking through Tibet this summer may be. This Venus is happiest knowing there's always more to discover about her partner and about herself.

This Venus sign's relationships must have that perpetual quality of growth, youth, and movement, too. Often people younger than us give us a charge because they see the world in a fresh way, but age is really just a state of mind. A closed mind gathers dust; an open mind is timeless and perpetually fresh. With your Venus in Gemini, you love to learn from the people you date, so you're often attracted to thinkers, teachers, writers, journalists—basically anyone who engages your curiosity and has a lot to say about a number of subjects. As long as your mind is engaged and your innate love for all things wonder-full is stimulated, you will feel happy and fulfilled.

CHANGING CHANGELING

One of Mercury/Gemini's many skills is shapeshifting. Mercury changes identities in the blink of an eye. Another Venus in Gemini I know, also a dancer, didn't come into her own until she began dancing with a troupe. This is no typical dance troupe; it's more like theatrical dance meets high-fashion runway. In front of a photographer or onstage, she morphs into character, a different one every time. Paradoxically, these costumes have the effect of making her look more like herself. In character, she's stunning. She comes alive.

To cultivate a charmed and dangerous Venus, as my friend did, the trick is to remain flexible, open, and scandalously flirtatious toward all of life. Astrologer Dana Gerhardt has said, "[Venus is] promiscuous with all of life…to enjoy it, play with it, surrender to it and create from it." The word "promiscuity" has been misunderstood and overused. By staying erotically and openly engaged with all of life, Venus is promiscuous with everything and everyone, but not necessarily in a sexual way. She is simply open to experiencing playfulness and adventure; she is open to the ever-present erotic life force pulsing through everything.

By now, Venus in Gemini, you've probably figured out who your soulmates are. They are interesting and interested in you, various and varied, and they are exciting to be around. Their bright intellects intrigue you, and they keep your head and heart spinning with new ideas, discoveries, and perspectives. Open-minded and curious, your Venus in Gemini partner is the one you're having fun with in this moment. That's the kind of person you could hang with for a very long time.

YOUR EROTIC STRENGTH

Marvel. Daily living is a never-ending episode on the Discovery Channel to you, because you're tuned in to all things amazing and miraculous. How many lives do cats really have? Are elephants the smartest animal? Does the spirit world speak, and what does it say? When you're inspired about your current fascination du jour, you have the wild enthusiasm of a kid in a candy store, your eyes as big as saucers, your heart and mind generously open. In fact, you'll sample a lot in life, and just when you decide on a favorite chocolate, philosophy, or track, you'll be off and running in a new direction. You want to try and taste everything. That's why being around you is endlessly exciting for others, for you bring freshness, childlike marvel, and perpetual wonder to your relationships.

IF YOU'RE IN LOVE WITH VENUS IN GEMINI...

Your Venus in Gemini will keep you entertained with witty stories, compelling conversation, good book recommendations, and flirty verbal banter—a form of foreplay for her. She needs an open-minded partner who won't judge her ideas and who arouses her intellect and mental curiosity. Your life with Venus in Gemini will be peppered with interesting observations and will never be dull.

Venus in Gemini is classically compatible with air signs (Gemini, Libra, Aquarius) and fire signs (Aries, Leo, Sagittarius). Pisces likes to talk, listen, and share their observations about the world as much as Gemini does, and Pisces' intuitive, feeling-oriented nature helps cerebral Gemini merge head with heart.

Venus in Cancer

The best and most beautiful things in the world
cannot be seen or even touched.
They must be felt with the heart.

~HELEN KELLER, VENUS IN CANCER

YOUR LOVE ELEMENT

Life-giving, nourishing, sustaining...this is water. Water is humble and unassuming and has a huge job to do. We know that nothing lives without water; all known life forms depend on it. After all, water is the source of all life. Water gives life by mediating reactions between organic compounds that allow reproduction to occur. Found in mother's milk and plasma—the nutrient-rich embryonic fluid of the womb—water is omnipresent wherever life is nurtured and sustained. Like a summer rain shower, water refreshes, forgives, and heals. We depend on water, rely on it, and not until we experience drought and famine do we truly value and give thanks to lifegiving water. Yet water understands, for just as the sea meets the shoreline, water always meets you where you are.

Your Secret Desire

To experience love as a safe haven, a lifelong connection based on kindness and unconditional love that allows you to let down your guard, share, and heal. As reassuring as a hug from an old childhood friend and as comfortable as your favorite PJs, this love feels safe and solid. Ideally it also includes plenty of heart-felt epiphanies, spiritual knowings, healing tears, meaningful mementos, crafty keepsakes, family heirlooms, and homemade cupcakes.

Your Love Charms

- Call the love therapist: you practice the power of unconditional love because you care. You can be crabby or feel unexceptional and still work miracles of the heart.

- You're a walking mood ring: the mood of the moment is written all over your face, making you a delightfully expressive and empathic partner.

- Your exotic changeability. Some days you're as predictable as apple pie and other days you're a wild-eyed chanteuse who throws reason to the wind. A Moonchild, you change with the Moon's phase and sign, and to the Moon you owe your subtle, unpredictable, and wildly romantic glow.

- Your feminine vulnerability. You're tender as a creampuff, even when hiding behind a tough-lady façade. You may not think of vulnerability as an asset, but notice how both sexes want to protect, cherish, and adore you for no reason at all. Your tender sensitivity endears others to you.

- Your whimsy and imagination. There's nothing more fun than following your whimsy—for a weekend getaway, thrift-store shopping, or a spontaneous cupcake-baking session for two. Bring on the romance!

- You practice "safe sex." When you feel safe and cared for, you're one of the most luminous, magical, and generous lovers of all twelve Venus signs.

- You create a safe haven for others. They know they can let down their guard, cry on your shoulder, and share difficult emotions with you.

YOUR LOVE GODDESS

Meryl Streep (b. 1949) has been called one of the greatest dramatic actors of all time. She is beloved for her ability to completely transform into her characters, her humor, and her ability to mimic different accents perfectly. It's impossible not to like Meryl, even when she plays the evil antagonist. With her twinkling laugh and gentle, wild-eyed Moon-face smile, no matter what character she inhabits, Meryl endears herself to us with her tender vulnerability, empathy, and whimsy—qualities of every Venus in Cancer.

It's difficult not to swoon. There's something enchanting about every Venus-in-Cancer born. That's because this Venus sign belongs to the feminine Moon—the planet of receptivity, romance, illusion, changeability, and mystery, the planet aligned with poets, lovers, and romantics. It's the magical Moon that makes coyotes yowl with hunger, lovers long for their true love, and sea creatures mate. Should she connect with you, this

Venus sign hints at the promise of coming into contact with these eternal Moon mysteries. Those with Venus in Cancer enthrall and enchant; when we come into contact with someone with this Venus sign, it's hard to know what mysterious spell we're under, but we do know we're spellbound.

This Venus sign can be as elusive, flirtatious, and mysterious as any other Venus sign at the beginning of a romance, but love for a typical Venus in Cancer is no lighthearted affair. This is an incredibly caring, empathic Venus sign who will walk to the ends of the earth for those she loves. The Moon, like Venus, is also a planet of love, but of a particular kind—nurturing, motherly love. Though by no means exclusive to mothers or women, this kind of love is easily observed in mothers. Imagine the vulnerable intimacy of a mother nursing her newborn child, the tender devotion, the feeling of being biologically bound to and responsible for someone else. This is how Venus in Cancer—a Venus sign for whom eroticism is very closely linked with caretaking and the biological urge to mate and nest—expresses love.

Forming a family, making a house a home, caring for others who need her, and being a domestic goddess bring so much pleasure, joy, and meaning to Venus in Cancer's life. These activities are historically feminine arts, so the Moon and Venus have another aspect in common: womanhood. Goddess lore gives three distinct phases of womanhood to the Moon, connecting each with a stage in the lunar cycle. The Virgin Maiden is a young new Moon, the Mother the full Moon, and the Wise Crone is the last quarter to balsamic Moon. We begin life as a fresh and innocent maiden. Venus in Cancer goes through phases as she moves from maiden to mother to wise woman, and while aging isn't easy for Venus, for Cancer, or for any woman, each new phase of femininity is pregnant with possibilities. At each phase of femininity, a Venus-in-Cancer woman harvests a new pearl of beauty and wisdom. This is true for Meryl Streep, who, in an industry notorious for ageism and sexism, has bucked the trend by still entertaining us in her wisdom years. Equally rare for Hollywood and apropos for Moon-ruled Venus, Meryl is sexy not because she is youthful or overtly sexual but because she is charming, whimsical, soft, empathic, and receptive—she is feminine, and that is sexy.

This Venus sign can feel torn between her home and her professional life. When she is pulled in both directions at once, negotiations will need to be made, but where there's love, there's a way. Meryl says, "I have a holistic need to work and to have huge ties of love in my life. I can't imagine eschewing one for the other." If Venus in Cancer leads a public life, she is also deeply private, choosing to keep her home a safe haven and keep her loved ones out of the fray. She knows the people and things that are most important to her are worth protecting.

Venus in Cancer can wear the look of a little girl lost (think Judy Garland, another Venus-in-Cancer-born woman), but through her devotion as a mate and/or mother, this Venus sign blooms. Unparalleled nurturing, tenderness, loyalty, and unconditional love—these are the gifts of the Moon. Will Venus in Cancer trust you enough to share her mystery, her love? She is one of the most vulnerable of all the Venus signs, and after she's been hurt, she keeps her heart under lock and key until it's safe to come out again. This Venus sign will need to learn to judge who she can safely let into her heart and who she can't. She knows there are wolves in sheep's clothing and no guarantees. But she also knows the only way to receive love is to open to it.

MOTHERLY LOVE

Many with Venus in Cancer will discover a previously un-tapped level of fulfillment through motherhood, but not all of you are born mothers. On a practical level, you possess maternal qualities—empathy, kindness, compassion, and unconditional love toward those in need—and while these qualities also fall under the umbrella of "mother," they're not exclusive to the role. You don't need to mother a biological child to tap your gifts. You might nurture a group of people, manage a team, or be a healing therapist who leads distressed psyches back home.

Just because she can become the quintessential mother archetype doesn't mean a Venus-in-Cancer born wants to be mistaken for your mother. Venus is not the Moon. She is not a convenience store, always open for business, 24-7. Venus generously gives, but she doesn't want to be taken for granted. You may see her in an apron, but she's just as likely to wear the sign you see in many people's kitchens: "Your mother doesn't work here. Clean up after yourself." This Venus sign may enjoy nurturing and ministering to those she loves, but she doesn't enjoy nurturing unhealthy dependencies in herself or others. Because she's so sensitive to others' energy, people with a lot of psychic baggage or demons are a real turn-off for her. Too much drama disrupts her sense of equilibrium.

The world can never get enough compassion and love, so this Venus sign is very much in demand. Her ruling planet, the Moon, is said to hold sway over the public mood, and this Venus often has her finger on the pulse of what people need and desire. Venus-in-Cancer born can be very popular—and very private. They need downtime to recover from their out-flow of giving and caring.

If you've got Venus in Cancer, the world needs your particular brand of love. Yet this Venus sign has the same problem as most mothers: though you are so gifted at giving and caring, you need to receive some care yourself. Spending time with other women, nurturing yourself at a spa, reading novels, and caring for and loving your body all serve this aim. After all, compassion begins at home.

Venus in Cancer might enjoy …

Hanging out at home, mood music, writing and reading, interior design, intimate dinner parties, being cozy, creative cooking, mysticism, baths, hydrotherapy, beaches, a beautiful bra, vintage anything, family photographs, lace.

There's No Place Like Home

Someone once said, "Every woman marries her father, and every man marries his mother." As unattractive a prospect as that is for some people, family is all-important to Venus in Cancer, and family dynamics often influence her relationships. Before starting a family of her own, she may need to look at her relationships in her family of origin, especially if those dynamics were troubling. By going back to the root source of her own home and family dynamics, Venus in Cancer better understands her own patterns and is freer to experience the love she knows exists in her heart, instead of what she's been shown.

What if we had great parents? Cancer charges the matrix of memory we've carried with us since birth, and Venus can gild our memory about our parents and make them into something better than they were. Nostalgia is a powerful aphrodisiac for

Venus in Cancer. Halle Berry, who has had a difficult time with relationships, once said, "I know that I will never find my father in any other man who comes into my life, because it is a void in my life that can only be filled by him."

Venus-in-Cancer born need to recognize the value of leaving home. Our loyalty to our mother or father can cause big problems not only in our choice of mate but in our committed partnerships. If good ol' Mom or Dad's opinion regularly enters into the conversation with our partner, and the ensuing antics are about as much fun as a trip to the dentist, we probably need to shift our family loyalties from our primary family to our partner. We may need to learn to stop seeking approval from our mom or dad, and stop attempting to care take of, placate, and please them. When we stop acting from learned attitudes, we can be a whole person in partnership.

Charlotte Kasl, in her book *If the Buddha Married*, holds that even though we may physically leave, we also need to psychologically break away from home, and this is a truly radical act. She writes, "[This] rite of passage involves becoming aware of the values they imparted to us and through a process of reflection and experimentation choosing which ones we want to keep and letting go of the rest." When we consciously choose what we want to take from our family of origin into our chosen one, we are free to experience a home and family of our own design.

MAMAS AND PAPAS

Although she can nest alone, Venus in Cancer generally won't want to. A mama bear needs a strong companion to accompany her through all the seasons—to help her make it through a lean winter, to yang her yin in the springtime, and to share the fruit of summer dreams. A mama needs a papa.

Since this Venus sign prides herself on creating a safe and secure nest, she needs a partner who offers a similar level of care and support so she can get to the business of being fancy and enchanting. There are a few Cancer crab traps she should watch out for. One classic trap is over-giving, caretaking, and trying to do it all yourself. This type of behavior sabotages her dreams of an equal love. Another crab trap? Choosing a partner who has a goodly amount of personal healing work to do always leaves this Venus more shell-shocked than healed. Such a person never allows Venus in Cancer to let down her guard enough to heal her own emotions, come fully out of her shell, and step into her own creative gifts.

Venus in Cancer is an enchanting siren, but without a nest to call home and a cast of supportive characters in her life, she may never step out from behind the shell and share her enchanting glory with you. To do so, she needs to feel safe, and to feel safe and secure, she needs a family…and a home. This "family" doesn't need to be biological, but it will include people who inspire in her a sense of true kinship and clan, and folks with whom she can let down her guard and feel safe and supported in doing so. Her home needs to be a retreat, a healing refuge from the insensitivity and unkindness in the world, and it will be filled with her own distinctive brand of femininity. From retro antiques to shabby chic, tea roses to a teapot collection, her home must always nurture her heart and spirit.

A mama needs a papa. What she gives she also needs to receive in kind, from a partner. Strong but not too tough, the right papa is tender, empathetic, and romantic—a person genuinely interested in settling down and forming a family, even if it's just a family of two. Venus in Cancer's soulmate is someone sensitive, nurturing, and kind; someone who will allow her to relax and to heal anything in need of healing. She needs a safe haven to thrive, so a protective, healing, nurturing, and even creative partnership makes sense for her.

THINK WITH YOUR VENUS MANTRA, VENUS IN CANCER

I am innately soulful, and so is my soulmate. I use my intuition, trust my instincts, and value my feelings by acting on them. I am endowed with tender compassion for others, but I'm also wise enough to know that being compassionate doesn't mean being a sucker.

SENSITIVE STUFF

Your heightened sensitivity is a gift, yet when an emotional scrape leaves you feeling like a truck just drove over your heart, you're tempted to believe that this lovely strength is a curse. It's not. With your Venus in Cancer, you are simply too sensitive to be put through an emotionally dramatic wringer of a relationship (in fact, you'd rather have your eyes poked out). Therefore, insensitive, insecure partners are not your type. This rule of thumb is even more valid the more sensitive you are.

When single, you would do well taking the time to get to know a potential partner; otherwise you might let your insecurity, combined with your deep longing for a partner who feels like home, guide you into making premature and wrong partnering choices. If you are looking for love outside of yourself before you've learned how to love yourself, you may attract a needy reflection of your own unhealed self—an emotionally immature or unstable partner who will eventually drive you nuts and lead you down a dangerous road of self-questioning and insecurity.

In a relationship, it's easy for you to play the mother role. You may fall into the arms of a partner who is still tied to Mama's apron strings—someone who expects you to do the traditionally feminine work (feeling, cooking, cleaning) and is all too ready to put you in the role of mother. Take care that household domestic duties are divided equally and your emotional needs are met, for your Venus sign is vulnerable to being the person who takes care of everyone else's needs and neglects her own.

Generally, Venus in Cancer finds it very satisfying to lend her friends and partners a shoulder to cry on, and she truly loves having someone to tend to and look after; but truth be told, she loves being looked after and emotionally supported even more. There's a touch of a parent-child dynamic in every Venus-in-Cancer relationship, which can be very fulfilling and sweet. There's nothing more healing than having a partner who will make you chicken soup when you're sick and tenderly soothe your fears. But tender loving care and devotion must be a two-way street. If one partner is always in the role of the parent and the other is always the child, that's not partnering—that's parenting.

Venus in Cancer is exceedingly practical and focused on making things work, but when the mood is right, she can be delightfully enchanting and fanciful. Moment to moment (for she is governed by the changing, mysterious Moon), the inner mystic, artist, poet, mythologist, comedian, and actor within this Venus sign will all emerge. While her circle of friends is often large and wide, few are invited into her private inner circle and considered close friends. The people with whom she feels safe enough to let down her guard, be fanciful, and get loony win her loyalty—and her heart.

TOUGH AND TENDER

Speaking of lunacy, lunacy soared in popularity during the romantic Victorian era, a time in history when uncomfortable emotions were pushed down into the feminine body rather than voiced, a time when many a woman fainted instead of raising her voice in a stifling, repressive atmosphere. Unfortunately, in those good old days it was much easier for a person to be called the crazy lady in the attic or to feign illness than to admit the more uncomfortable but glaring psychological and emotional truths about how she was really feeling. But times have changed. We don't have to shut down emotionally or act out psychosomatically when we have uncomfortable feelings. For this Venus, intimacy is an emotional experience, an exchange of feeling. Venus in Cancer needs to value all of her feelings and accept and share them with trusted others. After all, shared feelings, both positive and negative, open doorways to hearts.

Yet there are times when being emotionally transparent is like walking around with a sign on one's back saying "kick me!" Cancer is the sign of the Crab, and every Crab has a shell for a reason: self-protection. This Venus sign is more sensitive than most. She is too attuned to caring not to notice carelessness, too empathically attuned to supporting others not to notice self-absorption. The world is full of all kinds of people, people who can be self-absorbed and unkind. Even good people in moments of self-absorption and insensitivity hurt others. Venus in Cancer's defense against lapses of kindness is her shell. When she feels vulnerable and exposed like a walking nerve, when she knows she's in someone else's line of fire, it's time for the shell.

Once hurt, Venus in Cancer generally doesn't bounce back easily from relationship slights. She will put on her shell and hide out for a while. Friends and lovers may be concerned. Just give her time. She'll come out eventually. She knows she could hide forever, to protect her trust from being betrayed, her care and kindness from going unappreciated, her heart from being broken, but she's too much of a romantic softie to swear off love and connection. Instead, she will periodically don her tough shell when she needs healing, a retreat, or private time to spend in her imagination.

Life supplies those born with Venus in Cancer with plenty of dings, dents, and jostles from people who simply don't care and a family with an endless list of needs and demands. Sometimes we need to share our feelings—the good, the bad, and the ugly—with those we love. Sometimes we need to put on our shell and take care of ourselves. When Venus in Cancer feels the world go all bumpy, she can always pull on her magical Crab shell, become invisible, and go within—to reconnect, self-nurture, and heal.

Feminine Enchantments

Home and family are essential to understanding any planet in the sign of Cancer. This doesn't mean Venus in Cancer will have a house full of kids, and not everyone with this Venus sign is destined to be a parent. But she will want to have a family to nourish, tend to, and heal—even if family means two people and a couple of cats. A cozy Crab shack and a family unit she can call her own…there's probably nothing sexier for this Venus sign. Except perhaps a strong, able partner who will yang her yin, take care of her babies (pets or kids), and provide for the family.

Domestic bliss is a place that exists, because you go there often, Venus in Cancer. There are days when baking a good loaf of bread is the best therapy a girl could ask for, and when watching the Cooking Channel is the only form of relaxation that works for you. The kitchen? That is an erogenous zone rivaled only by the bedroom (when the bed linens are white, crisp, clean, and five-hundred thread count). Don't even get me going on how fun it can be for this Venus sign to buy pretty little things for her house.

You do love nesting, and at the end of a day of caring for others or making a creative contribution to the world, you do love having someone look after you. A candlelight dinner is great, but your real turn-on is being served by an attentive, tender, nurturing partner. When you feel cared for and protected, nurtured and supported, your soft, feminine beauty is set aglow. You become enchanting.

Your Erotic Strength

Intuition. You've got incredible intuitive radar, which you use on people and on shopping, too. I have a friend who says women have amazing "shopping intuition"—we seem to magically know when to pop into our favorite store, on the perfect day, and find the perfect little something on sale. Your erotic gift is kickin' intuition. A hunch, nudge, or whisper says something is off, or someone's had a bad day, or tomorrow's lunch date is going to cancel. You could be miles away from a loved one and intuitively know that something's wrong. This psychic sensitivity serves you well when it comes to knowing whether someone needs your tenderness or tough love. But like a spiritual muscle, you use it or lose it—"it" being the internal compass we all need to follow when internal alarm bells sound. Intuition can be ignored, so make sure to tune in to yours! Venus in Cancer has the kind of intuition that makes others wonder where she gets her inside information.

IF YOU'RE IN LOVE WITH VENUS IN CANCER...

Your Venus in Cancer brings an enchanting, warm glow of sensitivity, empathy, imagination, and warmth into your life. This Venus sign has strong instincts and desires for her home, so let her rule the roost; she intuitively knows how to create the right environment for your love nest. In you, she needs a tender, emotionally mature partner who values commitment and traditional values.

Venus in Cancer is classically compatible with water signs (Cancer, Scorpio, Pisces) and earth signs (Taurus, Virgo, Capricorn), but Libra or Leo could also be delightful. Libra shares Cancer's refined sensitivity and empathy, and the two could create a beautifully charming home and life together, while childlike Leo is adoring and adorable, drawing out Cancer's nurturing instinct and playful side.

Venus in Leo
♌

*When you stop putting yourself on the line
and you don't touch your own heart,
how do you expect to touch other people?*

~TORI AMOS, VENUS IN LEO

YOUR LOVE ELEMENT

Hot, brazen, passionate—fire animates all of life. Like a blazing hearth in the cold of winter, we become animated, enlivened, and warmed when fire arrives on the scene. Dramatic, expressive fire leaps, licks, and dances because it loves to be watched. Speaking in exclamations, it confidently takes up space: "Look at me!" "See what I can do!" Fire is theatrical and showy, glorious and proud. Fire warms and flatters. Ever notice how everyone looks better next to the light of a warm, glowing flame? Fire takes up as much space as you will give it, and then shares itself with you—generously offering its heat, light, and warmth to the tribe of humanity.

Your Secret Desire

To dare to spontaneously share yourself with another, with artistry, joy, humor, and a spirit of creative celebration. You have something original to offer the world, whether it's your generous affection and appreciation for others or an art form of your own design, and it's no secret that everyone you meet falls immediately and wildly in love (or at least really deep *like*) with you.

Your Love Charms

- Your signature style, which no other can replicate but everyone emulates. The stylish mark of creative authenticity is Venus in Leo's claim to fame.

- Your ardor for artistically creative people, things, and ideas. The birds and the bees, the children and the trees are all drawn toward your passionate enthusiasm.

- The way you make others feel adored, loved, appreciated, and seen. You have an air of royalty about you, and a royal holds on to her crown by being generous with her subjects and making sure they are acknowledged and happy.

- Your celebrity status, even locally speaking. You bring life to the party, any party, simply by showing up.

- You're entertaining. Quite the party in a box, you! In style and self-expression, you have a flair for the outrageous and are lively, classy, and elegant.

- Your good-natured sense of humor. Clowning around allows you to drop the everyday masks we all wear, and touch the hearts of others. You're willing to play the fool, which guarantees you'll never be anyone else's fool.

- Your ability to rip your chest wide open and bare your heart. You recognize that true love is impossible without risking your pride to be vulnerable with another.

YOUR LOVE GODDESS

The classy tastemaker Coco Chanel (Gabrielle "Coco" Bonheur Chanel, 1883–1971) was the It girl of her day, and her rags-to-riches transformation was nothing short of fabulous—just what you'd expect from a Venus-in-Leo woman! By being born with her Venus in Leo, the stage had already been set for Coco—she needed only to allow her unique creative potential to flow. Brilliant beauty is the fate of every Venus-in-Leo born who dares to share her creative gifts. This Venus's signature strength lies in generously sharing the vital life force she feels running through her creative and erotic being with the world. Coco did this with Leo flair, leaving her royal insignia "CC" on the fashion line still worn today.

The iconic woman we now know as Chanel was born in 1883 in a French poorhouse, where illiterate nurses who recorded her birth at city hall wrongly spelled her name Chasnel (Chanel with an "s"). As Coco's star rose, this error kept historians and curiosities at bay, allowing her to remain free from the stigma accompanying orphaned children at the time. Leo is the sign of royalty. Venus-in-Leo women are born with royal blood, but their life circumstances may betray this with humble beginnings or even hardship. Venus in Leo must always remember that she is a born queen.

In life, we are all asked to wear masks to survive. Often we learn rejection before acceptance and betrayal before trust, and we experience invisibility before we get a chance to shine in our strengths. Yet this Venus sign is of fixed quality, which is just an astrological term for "stubborn"! Through persistence and perseverance and by having confidence in her inner light, Leo persists—even when no one's applauding or noticing. Venus in Leo has the fortitude to keep on keeping on. Through the sheer force of her creative desire and focused intensity, this Venus sign has the magnetism to eventually manifest whatever it is that she wants. When the time is right for a Venus in Leo, any false masks she's had to wear will fall, and the real star will rise (as happened for Chanel).

Venus in Leo must be courageous enough to risk rejection—to perform, to write, to self-express. She must do that thing she loves to do, even if no one is watching (yet). She must do what she loves and risk remaining anonymous and unseen to do so, though once she takes that leap into her creative power, recognition soon follows. About her signature fragrance (now in every department store in the world), Coco once said, "This perfume is not just beautiful and fragrant. It contains my blood and sweat and a million broken dreams." Self-motivated and driven by creative desire and confidence in the value of her talent, Coco triumphed over insecurities that could have undermined her.

Chanel experienced hard times, yet she stayed true to her creative vision. When times are tough, a Venus in Leo must persevere and open her heart even wider. She must continue to create and love, and dare to trust in life just enough. She must not allow her fear of betrayal or rejection to stop her from shining, creating, loving, and sharing. With her artistic brilliance, she becomes the charismatic star who lights up a room. This is the fate of every Venus in Leo who dares to step into the spotlight of this Venus sign.

Chanel catered to no one's opinion of how a woman should dress, and so it was a bold and original move that inspired Chanel's LBD (little black dress) and the flapper look of the 1920s. No matter a woman's shape or wallet size, a well-designed LBD makes her feel special. This is a gift of a Venus in Leo, who is inclusive rather than exclusive. She will be generous with you, making you feel special. When Venus in Leo shines her spotlight on you, all eyes are on you. This is why fashion still worships at the altar of Chanel, as befitting a royal.

When Venus in Leo loves, she makes sure you know you are special because she knows how terrible it is to be ignored, unappreciated, and unseen. When she creates, she creates generously, channeling the forces flowing through her for the good of everyone, albeit in her own special style and way. Roll out the red carpet for Queen Venus in Leo, destined to make her own singular mark.

SPECIAL AND LOVED

Leo is ruled by the Sun, the star in our solar system around which all planets revolve. To be the center of a universe and fearlessly shine as bright as the Sun is what every Leo planet longs to achieve. Ancient cultures worshiped the Sun God, the star of Leo. They generously endowed great men and women with qualities of the Sun, like luminosity, greatness, charisma, strength, and fame.

This is why astrologers can say with confidence that if you have Venus in Leo, you are someone special. Of course, given the sheer number of Venus in Leos in the world (approximately one out of every twelve people), it would be impossible and ludicrous for all of them to be born into actual royalty. Yet all golden, fiery, creatively talented Venus-in-Leo women have one thing in common: they all descend from the royal astrological line of Lion goddesses.

If you are a Venus-in-Leo born, your mission is to create something fabulous while you're here and to shine brilliantly. That is your birthright. You may not want to rule the world as the almighty Sun does, but when you radiate your unique talents or creative contribution to the world, you feel confident and sun-kissed. Sunlight infused Coco Chanel's creative ambitions; her aesthetic shone through the clear, self-directed, and willful sign of Leo. It takes stubbornness and willfulness to see a vision through. The result was bright enough for all to see.

When Venus in Leo shares her creative gifts, she is truly a godsend to the rest of us. But what happens when she doesn't feel confident enough to share and create, or when there's no applause coming from the cheering section? When this Venus sign feels ignored or overlooked or her self-expression is checked by shame, her sense of gravity develops an unattractive wobble.

Leo is the archetype of kings and queens, and a queen must have a domain—an area of life that she "rules" and where she has creative dominion. Whether she is the queen of salsa class or the PTA, Venus in Leo must find a way to showcase her creative strengths, leadership, and artistry, or she and the people around her will suffer. Being ignored or feeling like a nobody is brutal for a Leo planet, but being taken for granted is even more painful. As astrologer Jeffrey Wolf Green says, "A Venus in Leo woman would rather die than be taken for granted." She must be an acknowledged queen, and she must ensure this by developing her creative gifts and valuing herself.

Venus in Leo might enjoy...

Celebrations, parties, fine dining, opulence, openheartedness, original style, bold colors, performance
art, live theater and concerts, performing, acting classes,
spending time with children, sporting events, being
spontaneous, sun chasing, sun worshiping.

LET THE LOVE FLOW

Leo is a surprisingly insecure, fragile sign. Many of us think,
*Oh Leo, they like being in the spotlight, so they must be comfort-
able with it.* Not true. In astrology, the signs we are born with
reflect the spiritual lessons we are trying to learn, and those
with Venus in Leo are working on trusting others enough to
share and express themselves—to finally come out of hiding
and play. In the karmic past, they may have been rejected for
simply being themselves, and the healing method for this is to
share their unadulterated true selves again, to spontaneously
share, play, trust, and love in the moment. After all, love only
opens to those who risk being their true selves.

If you want to woo a Venus in Leo, let the love, romance,
and luxury flow. This Venus wants to be delighted, surprised,
and a little spoiled. A Venus-in-Leo romance must start the
same as it remains throughout—a grand love affair. For the
entire duration of a relationship, Venus in Leo wants to feel
that every time is like the very first time. Whether she is with
her partner for twenty days or twenty years, she wants to be
adored and cherished and feel as playful and alive as a young kid
in love. A sexually exciting, amorous, fresh, spontaneous relationship is attainable: some people do wake up every morning
after twenty years excited to be next to the person they love!
For Venus in Leo, every morning needs to be like Christmas

morning. The golden stardust must never fade away. To some signs this may sound like a tall order, but it's necessary for Leo. She approaches relationships with an attitude of openhearted-ness, generosity, romance, playfulness, youthfulness, true and abiding love, and mutual respect.

To keep the love flowing, Venus-in-Leo born need to bask in the spotlight of adoration and affection; by receiving adoration and affection, they give the same to others. The quality of attention Venus in Leo offers her partners is neither vainglo-rious nor ego-stroking. She is generous, positive, enthusiastic, and kind, but like all Venus signs, she asks for the same quali-ties from her partner in return. She desires a constant feedback loop of creativity, warmth, and positive praise. She will happily do the same for you. Most importantly, while romance, playful affection, spontaneity, candor, and openheartedness color the initial stages of most love affairs, these must remain constant fixtures in the long-term relationship life of any Venus in Leo. Sure, it's fun, but this isn't all fun and games to her! Playfulness allows Venus in Leo to open up, to share, and, finally, to trust.

FIT FOR A QUEEN

Old astrology cookbooks of yesteryear have a habit of calling planets in Leo drama kings and queens. They like to paint Leos (or at least the Sun sign) as a narcissistic breed with megalo-maniac tendencies and superiority complexes. This is unfair to any planet in the sign of Leo, for they have to bear the brunt of this cliché, too. Acting holier than thou may be the shadow side of autocratic kings and queens, and it happens occasion-ally for Leo, but mostly it doesn't.

Still, Venus in Leo may recognize this tendency to create drama when she's feeling unappreciated, unloved, or ignored.

When a partner doesn't express appreciation for something she's done or she simply feels hurt, it's important for her to share that with the person. But Venus in Leo's pride can get in the way of opening her heart and sharing the pain she feels with her partner. She may instead stubbornly insist on her rightness, thereby trading an opportunity to be authentically vulnerable for dramatic fireworks. Too proud to show she's in pain or need, she lashes out and suffers for it. There's nothing sadder than a proud Lioness licking her wounds.

When this happens, how will you get what you want, Venus in Leo? Take a clue from your royal lineage. First, true royalty doesn't stay in power by lording over others; true royalty is generous and quietly dignified. Royals don't become royalty by treating others poorly; the opposite is true. Those who command our respect do so because we respect them, too. Problems also arise when we don't respect ourselves. If we don't treat our own desires, needs, and wants as legitimate by acting on them, if we think we need to ask someone else for approval or permission to get what we need, then we are not staying in our power as the queen.

Like all of us, Venus in Leo wants to be liked, appreciated, adored, and loved. She wants to feel special in the eyes of her lover—this is a totally worthy and human thing. But she cannot get the respect and love she wants through demands, drama, and diva behavior. The loving attention that flows to this sign quite naturally will happen when she trusts herself to authentically express and share her true feelings, without blame, judgment, or shame. There is no other way to get the love she needs. Demanding love and affection we feel we deserve but aren't getting is just another way of closing our hearts, and when that happens, we've left planet Love (Venus) for planet Ego.

THINK WITH YOUR VENUS MANTRA,
VENUS IN LEO

I embody divine inspiration by letting it ravish me as a lover would. I share my creative talents, and rays of beauty emanate from me, like sunbeams. As I generously praise and appreciate others, they do the same for me, and we raise the love vibration.

COMMONERS AND KINGS

Who is the perfect partner for a queen? A king, of course. A queen fares best with another royal as a consort. A queen is temperamentally suited to a strong partner to match her own strong, fiery nature. She is a leader, and she wants leadership in her partner. While a prince of a guy may make a great lover, her lifelong companion should be equally matched in creativity, talent, dynamism, and vision. What happens when she falls for the village cobbler, or the court jester, instead? Imagine our queen falling in love with a commoner to sense the potential for power plays and drama. The cobbler or court jester, insecure and threatened by the queen's power, lapses into moody, passive-aggressive behavior while the queen nags her would-be king to play a role he simply wasn't born to do.

No one wants this kind of drama. Venus in Leo needs to experience her own powerful strength, self-confidence, and self-assuredness through and in partnership. She needs to be matched by someone who neither lords over her nor is beneath her in stature and strength. Every Venus in Leo is blessed with the innate self-knowing and solar confidence of the Sun. If she wants to assume her rightful place in the center of the universe, she'll avoid the theatrics of an insecure partner and instead hire a chariot all the way to her Sun King.

SPONTANEITY AND JOY

Venus-in-Leo born are filled with the creative-erotic life force of the universe. That's why astrologer Jeffrey Wolf Green says Venus-in-Leo people are full of themselves! They are so full of selfhood that they are bursting at the seams to manifest something divine and delightful. And as a fixed (stubborn) sign, they are equipped with the persistence and drive to bring a creative vision to fruition. This Venus sign is stubbornly capable of manifesting magnificent beauties. She is the pulsing erotic center of all of life. Even if she doesn't communicate this, it will feel that way to her. Like a spring that gives rise to a golden fountain, within her bubbles the joy of all creation and of creating. It is her birthright to create something beautiful, something worth celebrating. What will she create?

There are paintings to paint, songs to sing, children to birth, and dresses to design. For Venus in Leo, a life well lived resembles a spontaneous champagne stream of self-expression, eroticism, playfulness, and beauty. Venus in Leo specializes in the art of living a life unscripted. She, more than any other Venus sign, enjoys abandoning herself to the moment. It's through being in this joyous moment, totally and fully, that she feels most beautiful and relaxed. She surprises even herself when she realizes she's the one lighting up the entire room.

For Venus in Leo, the secret to good living and good loving is cultivating spontaneity, joy, and creativity, rigorously and frequently. Whatever she does, it must be fun. Playtime with playmates is the essence of Leo joy. Her creative and social pursuits may sound like child's play to other signs, but fun, play, silliness, and creativity give her true self full-on permission to shine brightly and heal any shame or wounds surrounding her lovability and self-worth.

There's also healing in creative spontaneity. When we spontaneously share our innermost thoughts in conversation or take the stage to sing a song we wrote, we demonstrate to our deep self (the one who isn't sure whether it's safe to come out and play) that the world is a secure, good place to be. We need the same healing reassurance from our partners. When we get silly with our lover and they laugh, when we open our hearts and they smile, we finally start to believe in our lovability and self-worth, and we heal ancient wounds to those very same things.

SPECIAL LOVE

This Venus loves deeply, loyally, with heaping spoonfuls of generous attention and affection, fanfare and celebration. After all, when royalty comes to town, it's an occasion. Likewise, Venus in Leo specializes in *special love*. When she's "turned on"—generous with her attention, lavish with praise—those around her feel like the most attractive, beautiful, and brilliant people in the world. Others reciprocate in kind, and everyone basks in the warm glow of her special-love spotlight. But when that attention is lacking, no one feels special. Mystic teacher Stuart Wilde says, "Love is a quality of attention. It's a way of focusing on someone." Like all of us, Venus in Leo wants to be liked, appreciated, and loved, but a needy or insecure Lion can miss the Sun that is always there. Remember, Venus in Leo, you're no mouse; you're a Lioness! Your natural command is easy to access when you're in touch with your inner beauty, lovability, dignity, and self-worth.

Venus in Leo is an attentive and receptive lover. What makes a lover exceptional? Lovers express their affections forthrightly. Lovers get that adoring look in their eyes when they look at you. The best lovers know how to worship. They worship their beloved like the god or goddess they are. With spiritual generosity, physical demonstrativeness, and the flamboyance of a Casanova or a love goddess, Venus in Leo makes lovemaking exciting. Venus in Leo seduces with flair and artful style. Dressing up is fun, and so is role-playing and imaginary games of cat and mouse. Many Venus-in-Leo people like to be watched, so theatricality takes lovemaking to cinematic heights.

Venus's cardinal rule for happiness in relationship is: give and you shall receive. One of the best ways to get your partner to do your bidding is to give them the pleasure, affection, and attention you seek. Venus in Leo wants to be wooed in a particular way, and others want her wooing. How to woo? Heap attention and affection on her with gifts, concert tickets, kisses, and every Venus in Leo's dream: praise and affection. Give attention to get it.

No matter how evolved, grown-up, or egoless we think we are, none of us ever loses the need for recognition, praise, and applause. It's human nature. So when you're feeling low on your love meter, try this experiment at home.

Instructions: One person says the following to the other. Then switch seats.

I am your number-one fan. I love, applaud, and honor (list your partner's many talents here). You are blessed and beautiful in so many ways (list their beauty here). You are so fabulous, classy, brilliant, and original (insert other appropriately unique-to-them adjectives here), you blow me away! Your creativity is so endlessly prolific and astounding that I can't wait to see what you come up with next. In fact, sometimes you shine so brightly that people need to look away for fear of going blind. But I won't look away. I see all of you, and I love you.

YOUR EROTIC STRENGTH

Charisma. There's a type of beauty that's sold in a bottle and kept back-stocked on a shelf somewhere in a cold, lifeless department store. And then there's you—100 percent natural, vital, original, and alive *you*. Who needs cosmetics or Botox when you're a born Venus in Leo? You carry enough inner radiance to light up Times Square. You make other people feel pretty special, too. Hanging out with you makes others feel like they've entered a VIP club called Special, Worthy, Happy, and Loved. Trust the woo-woo, pop, and wow of your talent and creative gifts, your playful spontaneity and generous nature. Sun Goddess, your aura is golden, all-encompassing, and simply dazzling. This is true beauty.

IF YOU'RE IN LOVE WITH VENUS IN LEO...

Your Venus in Leo needs a relationship to be special and regal—no mere mortal love affair but a mythic, perhaps even once-in-a-lifetime event. Taking pride in each other is a form of love for this Venus sign, so prepare to be shown off (and show her off, too) and ditch the insecurity—she needs a partner with an equally strong ego. Venus in Leo will impress you with how fun-loving, colorful, and generous she can be, and while you don't have to do the same, you *must* appreciate her.

Venus in Leo is classically compatible with fire signs (Aries, Leo, Sagittarius) and air signs (Gemini, Libra, Aquarius) but finds an eager, appreciative audience in Cancer, who also brings out Leo's tender side. Leo discovers a mutual love for luxury, good taste, and pleasure in Taurus, who is happy to receive Leo's gifts.

Venus in Virgo
♍

We've got the gift of love, but love is like a precious plant.
You can't just accept it and leave it in the cupboard,
or just think it's going to get on with itself.
You've got to keep watering it.
You've got to really look after it…and nurture it.

~JOHN LENNON, VENUS IN VIRGO

YOUR LOVE ELEMENT

Peaceful, sensible, humble—earth asks for nothing. Perfectly at peace, earth holds everything in balance while the human race does its crazy dance. Earth silently and generously supports us, providing all the raw materials we need for life on Earth. Occasionally we revere our planet—for instance, during a sunset that takes our breath away. We might appreciate the abundance she provides and give thanks. We may make a conscious choice to be kind and do no harm to the planet that serves us in myriad ways and asks for so little in return. Earth absorbs every action we take on her behalf, be it great or small. Earth silently notices everything.

Your Secret Desire

To bring the perfection of Heaven down to Earth. You were blessed with the ability to see the difference between what is and what could be, as well as the know-how to bridge that difference. Through your art, your craft, through loving someone well, you will make this world and the people in it better.

Your Love Charms

- Your humble heart. Through facing your inner demons—all the ways you tell yourself "I could be better"—you humbly and persistently work on purifying your heart. Your relentless self-examination and humility make others trust you.

- Your fanciful and practical connection to the natural world. Nature itself is a magical place brimming with possibilities. You are as rapturous over a dewy rose on your morning walk as you are about your medicinal rose hip tea.

- Your savvy. Whether organizing a flow chart or a food drive, designing a dress or public policy, life runs more smoothly with you around.

- You're whip smart. Blessed with a quick wit and intelligence, some of the most hilarious people are born under your Venus sign.

- Your eagle-eyed vision. Whether facing a struggling relationship or getting rid of garden pests, you can reduce a problem to its simplest common denominator.

- Your good taste. You can spot a fake a mile away, making you a great shopping partner and an excellent judge of character. You have an eye for craftsmanship and quality.

- Natural elegance. You're always looking for efficient, easy ways to smooth the wrinkles of the world, and as a result you embody the elegance you strive to create. Elegance becomes you.

YOUR LOVE GODDESS

Like Botticelli's *The Birth of Venus*, Venus in Virgo materializes out of the mists of the eternal—ethereal and lovely, a beautiful apparition and a sight to behold. If there was a soundtrack to Venus in Virgo descending to Earth, it would be the music of an angelic choir. In this Venus, we behold the compassion of Mother Mary, the sanctified sensuality of a sacred harlot, and the wisdom of a high priestess. Earth shocks this Venus. It is often a violent, crazy-making planet. It can be a beautiful and lovely garden of paradise, to be sure, but being human is one of the more difficult assignments given to any soul, and the Virgo angels know it.

And so Venus in Virgo weeps and mopes around for a few days, feeling unhappy and sorry for her predicament. Then she rolls up her sleeves, because she knows in her heart that she wasn't sent here to relax but to grow spiritually. She senses that she has something to contribute, that she can make the world a better place, an easier, kinder, more beautiful place. The angels are rooting for her. They also know that the rigorous growth this Venus sign undertakes for her spiritual development is monumental. So they bless her with a few key gifts: a strong backbone, whip-smart intelligence, and a superb ability to find and solve problems.

Such qualities you share with your heroine, Eleanor Roosevelt (1884–1962), a woman of can-do and candor who was voted "the world's most admired woman" in international polls again and again. In true form, Eleanor wasn't born with the unwavering, tough-as-nails persona we associate with her—she worked hard for it. Eleanor's confidence wasn't a given; it was earned. As a child, Eleanor regarded herself as ugly. (Venus is the planet charging self-esteem and beauty.) Even as a child, she was a serious, old-fashioned type. Those born with Venus in Virgo find it easy to focus on their physical flaws. A biographer describes Eleanor's childhood as one of insecurity in which she was starved for affection. This is the same woman who coined the phrase "No one can make you feel inferior without your consent." Nevertheless, even at age fourteen, Eleanor understood that "no matter how plain a woman may be, if truth and loyalty are stamped upon her face all will be attracted to her." Eleanor began forming intelligent assumptions that would characterize her remarkable life.

Self-respect and self-worth—every Venus sign needs these in order to make intelligent relationship choices, to be happy. For Venus in Virgo, self-love, worthiness, dignity, and self-pride are not freely given. A Virgo planet can take nothing for granted; it must earn everything. Venus in Virgo figures the only way she can truly possess rock-solid self-worth is through critically assessing everything she is and is not. Humility helps. Self-acceptance in the face of her own inscrutability proves to be a great teacher. Her goal is to attain unbreakable confidence in herself—the confidence of Eleanor Roosevelt.

Venus in Virgo has a job to do, and she has the persistence and determination to get it done. She may use her pragmatic vision and desire to make the world a better place in her profession. Work is one reliable method Venus in Virgo uses to work on herself; as she consistently improves her skills and becomes better at what she does, she feels more competent as a person. Partnership also presents the opportunity to work on herself and, whether professional or personal, is also a vehicle for self-perfection. Eleanor Roosevelt's marriage, her husband's presidency, and even his paralysis gave her eagle-eyed acumen a true vocation, a calling. Partnership afforded her the opportunity to make a political and personal contribution. Even though Franklin accused her of having an unyielding nature ("Your back has no bend," he once told her), her backbone was enviable.

So it goes for Venus in Virgo. She doesn't do "easy," but she sure knows how to roll up her sleeves and get things done. Through self-reliance and raw determination, Eleanor Roosevelt became a confident woman who was admired and loved by many, and who made a difference in the world. She achieved confident self-possession and self-worth, the aspiration of every person born under this Venus sign.

GODDESS WORK

She may be a closet analyst or may enjoy organizing closets, but to be happy, Venus in Virgo needs to get to work. Virgo is the sign of the servant, analyst, and craftsperson. Her driving desire to improve is put to work in service of making the world a better place. With her penchant for perfection and her proclivity for planning, organization, and flawless execution, she patiently and methodically works to manifest her ideals, values, and vision. Whether she's starting a designer shoe company or improving her relationships, when there's something to work on or work out, there's no one more devoted to making things work.

Venus in Virgo was born with exacting intelligence; she possesses the smarts to fix problems and find solutions, to troubleshoot waylaid plans and set things straight. Yet that same eagle-eyed creative intelligence that so clearly sees what's wrong in order to make it right can be disabling for the easy, breezy style of Venus. No other sign is more apt to focus on the little things and people that annoy her. When Venus in Virgo focuses on what's wrong, she can find it hard to relax and simply enjoy life, and she may even lose all perspective on what's truly important in life. Yes, Venus in Virgo is often guilty of missing the forest for the trees.

This is hard on the goddess of pleasure, for she is the part of us that lives to love and laugh. How can Venus in Virgo ever relax and enjoy life when she gets carried away so easily by her less-than-perfect vision? The only thing Venus wants to get carried away by is laughter, a tickle fest, and a gallon of ice cream.

By finding flaws in the people and world around her, this Venus can feel blessed with her supreme knowledge and claim superiority over others. Equally, she can turn her critical eye on the person she sees in the mirror, regarding her Goddess-given features as flaws and her body with disdain. When Venus in Virgo becomes dissatisfied with who she sees in the mirror, she becomes unhappy, negative, hypercritical, and uptight. An unhappy Venus in Virgo is no fun for anyone.

Focusing her exacting vision outside of herself and onto an art form, a personal growth project, or a craft helps. The secret for Venus in Virgo lies in knowing that the best way to work out her drive for growth and perfection is through working on something important and external to her. Whether she's designing clothes or baking the perfect brioche, as she humbly hones her craft—a process whereby screw-ups and failures are built into successes and victories—she humbly perfects herself.

Through focusing all that perfecting, analytical energy outside herself and onto the world where it is needed, Venus in Virgo learns buoyancy. What's buoyancy? It's the difference between jumping into the deep end every time you see something "not quite right" versus being able to ride the waves of life with a general sense of well-being. When we master buoyancy, we have a peaceful, easy feeling that we are doing just fine, no matter how low or high the tide.

Venus in Virgo might enjoy…

Cleaning, organizing, superior craftsmanship, pets, planners, sorting and folding laundry, nature, contemplation, earthy scents and oils, white linens, a tailored wardrobe, a charitable cause, self-help books, spiritual books, relationship workshops.

THE DETAILS OF LOVE

Yours is a practical earth Venus sign. In layperson terms, this means you prefer tangible efforts in love over flaky promises, "maybe tomorrows," and fantastic notions. You admire people who have know-how and demonstrate strong ethics. You like to keep it real. Yours is the sign of wise discernment, and when healthy and whole, you have unusually strong boundaries with others. This means you aren't necessarily dependent on anyone, for you are the *virgin* goddess, which in the original sense of the word means whole and complete unto yourself.

Venus in Virgo makes herself indispensable to others because she likes to help. This Venus can easily put others' needs first, but she must be recognized for her efforts—appreciation expressed for a job well done, a wonderful homemade dinner, or remembering to pick up the laundry are all great options.

Gary Chapman, author of *The Five Love Languages*, says there are five different love languages, and problems arise in partnership when we don't speak or understand our partner's love language. Some people show love through gift-giving, and others through time spent together or physical touch. Venus in Virgo shows love through acts of service. Showing up on time, making an extra effort, following through on your word—these are all loving gestures that will never go unnoticed by Venus in Virgo. For this Venus sign, actions always speak louder than words.

This is a clue about how to keep your love alive in the long-term. With your Venus in Virgo, you need a soulmate who speaks your love language, one who values follow-through and shared responsibilities as much as you do. You need to share the mundane, ordinary events of the day with someone who is genuinely interested, from how you spend your time day to day to the new project you've picked up. For someone who equates love with attentiveness, and devotion with careful consideration, love is in the details. In our fast-paced world with so many things competing for everyone's attention, that's a tall order. Your ideal partner is ultra-attentive and sincerely interested in how you're doing; thus, someone with their Sun, Moon, or rising sign in Virgo would be a good match for you.

Almost Perfect

Like a master craftsperson, you live to create a perfect, beautiful love or art form. The Venus-in-Virgo quest for perfection can drive you relentlessly and successfully toward self-improvement and personal growth. When taken to an extreme, you can become a taskmaster, appearing cold or unloving, which is the diametric opposite of who you truly are. When this energy dominates a less-than-perfect relationship, the partnership itself can become a perpetual thorn in your side.

More than any other Venus sign, yours analyzes and frets and worries over the state of her relationships. If there's a problem, you'll be the one to find it. The thing is, every rose has its thorns. That's how the Creator made roses. Likewise, you need to embrace the fact that the sweet bloom of love will often also be thorny. If you focus on the thorns, you'll never notice the blooms. To grow your love patch into a prize-winning rose garden, you must consistently and diligently widen your focus. Notice the little things you've overlooked. Notice the fullness and sweetness of the good in your life. Otherwise, you'll miss the ecstasy for the agony—a tragedy.

In praise of imperfection: humans are imperfectly perfect. The Great Creator obviously has a different definition of perfection, as he/she regularly creates anomalies (babies born with birth defects, genetic diseases, etc.) in his/her image. If perfection is part of the divine plan, then perfection cannot be an absolute state but a spiritually evolving one that helps us to learn lessons that only imperfection can teach. Those lessons may be deeply personal to each of us, but it appears that imperfection motivates our spiritual growth as humans. If everything were already buttoned up and worked out, why would we reach for more?

Think about this: as a Venus in Virgo, accepting your own perfect imperfection may be your most challenging work and your most generous act of self-compassion. If you struggle with perfectionism, try scheduling regular "let it go" days. Pick one day a week to be messy, chaotic, and imperfect—by design.

By accepting that imperfection has a place in the master plan, you help us to accept that we, too, are already beautiful, beloved, and imperfectly perfect.

THINK WITH YOUR VENUS MANTRA, VENUS IN VIRGO

I completely and totally accept myself, even when the other person is wrong and I'm right, and when I'm wrong and they're right. Today I choose not to sweat the small stuff and to remain happy instead. I offer the best of myself and look for the best in others.

THE WORTHIEST

No Venus sign likes to be taken for granted, yet because Virgo is so competent, she often takes on more than most and never asks for credit. Unlike the zodiac sign before her, Leo, who carries herself like a queen, Venus in Virgo inwardly feels like a grain of sand on an endless beach. She often has self-doubt about her personal worth and is inclined to play down her efforts, which only adds salt to the wound. This is a shame, because whereas some other Venus signs are guilty of too much marketing and not enough substance, Virgo's attentiveness, precision, and dedication toward improving make her good work the worthiest.

Virgo is a sensitive, hardworking, and humble Venus sign. However, humiliation (shame) can mask itself as humility—and they are not the same. Low self-estimation may plague this Venus sign in ways she doesn't easily understand, so she may work harder than necessary to make things right and perfect in the world, and with others, and thus she makes things harder on herself than they need be. Atoning for personal faults and inadequacies by serving time in an abusive or codependent partnership is an expression of this. Not asking for what it is we really need and want from our partner because we think we don't deserve it, or we think they're unable to give it, reflects low self-worth. This isn't unworkable—nothing is for this Venus sign! To change this pattern, she needs to improve herself while not making herself wrong in the process. Venus in Virgo needs a partner who will not underestimate, shame, or criticize her or make her feel inadequate, but more importantly she must stop doing that to herself.

When Venus in Virgo accepts the difference between where she wants to be and where she is, and humbly works toward that, her humility is attractive. Her easy competence; the way she makes herself indispensable to a cause, creature, or person; her generosity of time, energy, and kindness—what's not to love?

Tend Your Love Garden

There is a reason this Venus sign needs to use relationships as a vehicle for growth. In the karmic past, relationships didn't allow her to develop as a person, and it stunted her true capacity. Venus in Virgo got bored, and served time in a dead-end relationship. Just as a flower can grow only as much as the environment and the people in it allow, perhaps in the karmic past Venus in Virgo never figured out how to create the right conditions for growth, or they truly didn't exist. Unwittingly, or by her own hand, Venus in Virgo was a flower held back by nutrient-poor soil.

With your Venus in Virgo, this may have left a karmic residue of feelings: disappointments, fears, and anxieties about a partnership you believe is holding you back, or feelings that don't actually match the choices that exist in your life today.

Today, you must move beyond feelings of dissatisfaction and into practical action. If you've experienced relationships that stifled you or clipped your wings, the challenge today is to grow. You must claim your need to have the love you want and, if necessary, wrest it from your current partnership and start changing its dynamics. Imagine two people facing seemingly insurmountable issues and slogging away at them on a daily basis—that's Venus in Virgo. The key to romantic happiness, for you, is to constantly work on today's relationship.

When dissatisfaction arises, Venus in Virgo must identify and tackle it with equal parts tenacity and love, because untended weeds are unforgiving—they can overtake a beautiful garden virtually overnight. This Venus's vigilance must include not letting grievances pile up, not allowing the petty things to consume the love, and handling the relationship's responsibilities—the duties and roles that come with partnership—with efficacy and clearly defined roles. For Venus in Virgo, love is expressed through mutual responsibility to the partnership and each other's happiness. With this shared commitment, the partnership thrives.

If you're a Venus-in-Virgo born, there are always two choices: be unhappy or roll up your sleeves and get to work. A Venus-in-Virgo partnership must be based on rigorous mutual growth. A real relationship is not a cakewalk; it takes work. Venus in Virgo can create a loving partnership that works, knowing it's effort and time well spent.

VIRGO, HEAL THYSELF

Venus in Virgo is a mistress of contradictions, for there are two competing realities living inside her: (1) how she wants the world to be, and (2) how it actually is—or the way things are and the way they could be if things were perfect. This chasm motivates Venus in Virgo to be genuinely helpful, and she often is. Yet when the standards she holds aren't flexible and she puts too many conditions on others, they are bound to fall short (and be genuinely annoyed). To avoid alienating others, it pays to be discerning about who receives her eagle-eyed attention—namely, the many people and things in this world that both need and want her help.

An art or craft, a career, her communication skills, finances, body, and health...all are excellent vehicles for perfecting. It could take some time, but she's an earth sign, so she was born with persistence. She isn't afraid of rolling up her sleeves and tackling something that appears too tedious to others (she actually enjoys detail-oriented work that others don't). Yet before she changes the world, she's got to clear up any misconceptions she may have about her worthiness.

Venus in Virgo, you already possess the resources you need to be happy. The motivation and methods are contained within each Venus sign. If unhappiness, shame, or inadequacy plague your relationships and self-worth, this also motivates you to address these issues, to grow. Frankly, you don't need to know why you suffer from a sense of inadequacy or why you feel stifled by a relationship. In fact, there is a saying often heard in twelve-step recovery programs: "*Why?* is not a spiritual question." *Why?* is a question that keeps you in your mind. The overly analytical, questioning mind—the mind that separates us from Spirit—is the same mind that keeps Venus in Virgo up during sleepless nights.

Venus in Virgo's motto is: if it isn't growing, it's broken. However, if this sounds like a tall order, a spiritual perspective and practice can help nurture an attitude of kindness, gentleness, and acceptance. By addressing in practical terms the difference between what you want your relationship to be and what it will take to get there, you can find the happiness you deserve. You can make peace with the fact that perfection is an impossible destination. And you can take bittersweet pleasure in knowing that of all the Venus signs, you get the closest to perfection, with equal parts self-love and elbow grease.

YOUR EROTIC STRENGTH

Sacred sensuality. The Virgin is the original chaste babe—pure in spirit and divine in flesh. As a card-carrying member of the Goddess tribe, at a time when civilization held the lifegiving, creative powers of the feminine in high regard, the sacred harlot made love to battle-weary soldiers, healing and renewing their spirits with her feminine energy, and ritually renewed her body-mind-spirit at secret mountain spring meetings with her goddess sisters. Even when betrothed, this Venus sign remains the self-possessed Virgin, pure and whole unto herself. You benefit from returning to these ancient sacred practices of sensual renewal. Restore your goddess self in nature, by sacred pools; spend time with women friends and with animals. Humanity needs less feminine shame and more shameless abandon. Share your sacred sensuality and be the goddess you are!

IF YOU'RE IN LOVE WITH VENUS IN VIRGO...

This Venus sign loves to feel indispensable, helpful, and competent, leaving you to wonder how you ever got along without her. Venus in Virgo craves a relationship that constantly grows and evolves, so expect occasional outings to Tony Robbins events and couples workshops, where your attentiveness will be duly noted (these will be followed by discussions). Keep the embers of love burning a long time time by being as dedicated to nurturing the healthy growth of your partnership as you are to your partner.

Venus in Virgo is classically compatible with earth signs (Taurus, Virgo, Capricorn) and water signs (Cancer, Scorpio, Pisces), though expansive, philosophical Sagittarius is a wise choice, offering Virgo plenty of food for thought, a plethora of fresh perceptions, ideas, and adventures.

Venus in Libra

The idea of my life as a fairytale is itself a fairytale.
~GRACE KELLY, VENUS IN LIBRA

YOUR LOVE ELEMENT

Balancing, flowing, harmonizing—air holds the universe in balance. Inhaling and exhaling the breath, or prana (the "breath of life"), vitalizes and balances our life force energies. Bringing the yin and yang movements in our lives into equilibrium is a balancing act, but air makes it look so easy and effortless. We gracefully stay in balance by receiving rich, life-giving oxygen with the in breath and by giving our carbon dioxide to the trees and plants on the out breath. Receiving and giving, action and rest, independence and relatedness—one follows the other as naturally as respiration. Every meditation practice returns to the breath, because when we breathe easy, no matter how crazy the world is, we achieve perfect balance.

Your Secret Desire

To meet your heavenly match, your equal in every way. Your ideal partner will value you in the way you wish to be valued, graciously accept the copious amounts of support and affection you offer, and dignify and elevate you in the same way you so naturally dignify and elevate them. Your perfect match never falls from a too-high pedestal, because you're standing as an equal, right there beside them.

Your Love Charms

- Your elegance and sophistication. You could take tea with the Prime Minister of the United Kingdom and outshine him with your good graces, effortless calm, and poise.

- Your judicious sense of right and wrong. Whether it's a dispute over foreign policy or what to eat for dinner, others can count on you to be fair and impartial.

- Social intelligence. You could write a book on how to sensitively say what needs to be said without stepping on anyone's toes.

- Your cool self-composure. Exhibiting grace under pressure, no matter how stressed you may be, you convey the impression of having it all together.

- Empathy. It's easy for you to walk in another person's shoes. This has the effect of making others feel utterly understood by you.

- Making it (love, art, looking good) look so easy. You always come across appearing unruffled and put-together. How do you do it?

- You're nice—the kind of nice that smooths over awkward social moments and finds common ground with uncommon people. Like a smile, nice never goes out of style.

Your Love Goddess

Hundreds of weddings take place every day, but one royal union extended beyond the personal realm: the marriage between Grace Kelly (1929–1982) and Prince Rainier III affirmed the collective belief that true love exists, that "the one" is out there. Hers is a classic story, a tale of a Philadelphia-born girl next door who was raised by hardworking parents from immigrant families and married a prince. It was a match seemingly made in heaven. Grace's marriage demonstrated what every Venus in Libra knows: that true love exists, and when you find your perfect other half, anything is possible.

Grace Kelly, a natural-born princess possessing Venus in Libra's innate sophistication, had the ability to lubricate the wheels of social interaction with tact, diplomacy, and grace. Like a diamond whose facets reflect the light of those around it, Venus in Libra's natural leadership skills shine in the company of others, where she is utterly at ease, relaxed, and in command. Guiding social conversation and interactions like the choreographer of a great ballet, she is socially adept. From smoothing over awkward moments to sensing exactly when to speak and when to listen, from choosing the perfect joke for an occasion to knowing when to steer away from inappropriate topics that would make others uncomfortable, Venus in Libra is her most charming and disarming in the company of others.

Venus rules two signs, Taurus and Libra. Libra is the airy, mental side of Venus. A social strategist, a tastemaker with sophisticated ideas, and a sucker for romance, this Venus sign doesn't always swoon over romantic comedies and royal weddings, but she loves love and lives to relate. Venus in Libra is seeking her perfect complement, intellectually, spiritually, socially, and aesthetically. Call her idealistic, but don't call the pursuit farfetched. This is the Venus sign of the original mighty Aphrodite. Venus in Libra is looking for the ideal mate, a meeting of minds as much as hearts, and she will find that person.

As such, relationships may be all-consuming at times and may even appear to define her. This Venus finds it difficult to be alone—which is why this Venus sign rarely is. Grace Kelly dated and received proposals from quite a number of big names before she married. Venus in Libra needs social stimulation, which courtship provides, but generally a Venus in Libra wants to be in one long-term, committed partnership. Libra rules the institution of marriage, and it's in marriage that we learn how to compromise and negotiate our roles and desires with each other. We learn that while our points of view may be different, they don't have to be mutually exclusive. You may say "tomato" and I say "to-mah-to." You may prefer rock music while I think rap is better. Yet for a marriage to work, at the end of the day we must know no one person is right. Venus in Libra can do one of the hardest things required of us in marriage: she easily tolerates the paradox of loving and supporting another without necessarily having to agree with the person.

Grace's marriage catapulted her to a whole new level of personal growth and possibilities. A Venus-in-Libra born probably invented the art of marrying well, which is more than knowing that the right relationship can open social or professional doors—though it can do that. A great relationship—with a person who complements your strengths and buttresses your weaknesses—can make you, while a partner who holds you back can break you. The ideal partner plays to our strengths and supports our personal growth and success. The right partner opens doors we never could have opened on our own.

Grace Kelly was the epitome of class, ease, and elegance. On the day she married Prince Rainier III in the Throne room of the Palace of Monaco in a storybook wedding televised to millions throughout the world, the collective heart of love deeply exhaled...ahhhhhh. Grace reaffirmed the myth we all are born believing and the one many of us chase to the very end of our lives: that somewhere out there, there is someone for every one of us to love.

HAPPILY EVER AFTER

It's the best part of the story. You know, the part where the prince and the movie star live happily ever after. Did the starry-eyed couple, the Rainiers of Monaco, live happily ever after? There's inference and there's opinion, and frankly there's no telling. After her marriage, Grace stopped acting and Prince Rainier banned her films from being shown in his country. The princess never made public comments. Venus in Libra never airs her dirty laundry in public, so she would be the last to say, but we can question her union's fulfillment based on astrology.

This Venus sign is socially sensitive, but the public image of Venus in Libra's partnership may not always match its reality. Like a wedding cake that is all frosting and no substance, this Venus can appear to have a perfect relationship, valuing the partnership for what it provides materially, aesthetically, and socially even if it lacks satisfaction at its core. Why? Just as Aphrodite in her magic girdle transformed herself into any person's desire, this Venus can favor what others want for her to the point of giving up important pieces of herself—her very identity—to her partner.

Belonging to the country club, living in a house with a white picket fence, and being the proud partner of an upstanding person in the community are all fantastic, but if being with her partner forces Venus in Libra to compromise her very essence and freedom, that price is too high. Did Princess Grace make a bargain with the Devil? We may never know. But for this idealistic Venus sign who strives for material, social, and professional success through partnering, there's nothing more satisfying than having the image match the reality.

LOVE STRATEGY

Whether or not you have Grace Kelly's movie star looks, there's something sophisticated and charming about every Venus in Libra. Even if you're not aware of it, something inside of you—Venus—is sending out a receptive signal to potential partners that says, "Let me show you how fantastic your life will be with me in it."

This is the Venus sign of irresistible personalities such as Hugh Grant and Rita Hayworth, people known for their social charms. Venus in Libra is intelligent, loves learning, and is willing to expend effort on people she likes and wants to impress—and she does. She impresses them with the thought of how wonderfully sweet their lives could be together.

Venus in Libra is charming, polite, and nice, but don't mistake her for being weak-willed. "Libra has an iron fist in a velvet glove," or so say astrologers of the sign of the balancing Scales. Libra has a way of getting what she wants, and she does this by being pleasing and attempting to give others exactly what they most desire. As is the case with a masterful peacemaker, politician, or princess, diplomacy is second nature to Venus in Libra, and at the end of the day she recognizes that through being seductive, compromising, and pleasing, she will get what she wants. She does this with or without the other person's conscious awareness.

She does enjoy making peoples happy, knowing it is to her advantage to make sure you are, because generally speaking, if you're not happy, she's not either. But this Venus sign can be as calculating and strategic as any military general. If she wants you or wants something from you, she'll find out what you most desire and then give it to you. Soon she'll have you eating out of the palm of her lovely hand.

Venus in Libra might enjoy...

Matchmaking, socializing, making art, museum and gallery openings, beauty treatments, shopping, design, giving gifts, libraries, reading, learning, counseling others, yoga, partner dancing, flower arranging, beautiful dresses, fashion, taking time to relax.

BALANCE AND PLEASURE

Like a ballet troupe performing a dance, it takes diverse and numerous people to pull off a grand performance. As though directing a ballet, you easily see the interdependence of life and its dancers. With your Venus in Libra, you see the role each person plays in the grand scheme of things, which makes you a natural leader among others—you know how to keep the dance running smoothly and the dancers *en pointe*. Staying in regular contact with people and remembering birthdays and social events keep your alliances strong, which will help you to get what you want—future collaborations, invitations, pay raises, dates—later. When there's conflict, you can smooth ruffled feathers with charm and tact, guiding people toward peace, love, and understanding with your stellar leadership skills.

Relationships aren't always a breeze for you, though. Venus in Libra has oodles of empathy, and that, combined with a desire to please others, can make it challenging to get your own needs met. Your partner's influence and opinion about you matter, but they shouldn't matter so much that you compromise yourself.

When the easy allegiance and support you give others is at the expense of yourself, it's a sign to pull back and re-center. Balance is an evolutionary strategy for Libra. Like a tightrope walker, this Venus knows that staying true to herself while keeping another happy is a delicate art. Wavering on her tightrope, she finds balance elusive. She learns to periodically re-center, turn inward, and reconnect with herself and then return with self-awareness to the partnership.

To re-center, this Venus needs to relax. In ancient myth, if Venus wasn't on the prowl, she was just having a good time being social. This goddess relaxes by socializing, but Venus in Libra may find it necessary to take a break from the exhausting circuitry of relationships and socializing in order to rest. Harmony, peace, beauty, and relaxation should be part of her everyday life. Regular cultural outings exposing her to diverse people, places, and ideas; favorite peaceful environments to relax in; a beautiful home with tasteful art, adornments, and simple luxuries—these are not only Goddess-sent but are necessary for her well-being and happiness. As she cultivates harmony in the outer world, she experiences it within and then radiates it.

The Power of Two

Will Smith and Jada Pinkett Smith. Gwyneth Paltrow and Chris Martin. Hillary Clinton and Bill Clinton. Georgia O'Keeffe and Juan Hamilton. Prince Charles and Princess Diana. At least one half of each of these power couples has (or had) Venus in the sign of Libra (both Will and Jada have Venus in Libra). It's no mistake that each found themselves in a power partnership. Venus in Libra should aim high and set her standards on someone who mirrors the best in herself. Why? It's the secret of her success. What she wants to accomplish in life cannot be done alone.

For Venus in Libra, so much hangs in the balance when it comes to choosing the right partner. To be with a well-matched partner is probably one of the greatest sources of pleasure and joy for Libra, which is why being with the wrong person is so costly. A partnership with anyone less than an equal is brutal for this Venus, who thrives on mutuality and the perfect collaboration of strengths and weaknesses.

The Venus-in-Libra relationship resembles a union that thrives on the same principles as any democracy: worth, respect, and the pursuit of happiness for each individual and the necessity for occasional compromise. There's no room for power-trippers or domineering types in a Venus in Libra's life; a Libran relationship always makes a place for both people. Ideally, the two people should fit together like a puzzle; what the other lacks, the other brings. For instance, you write amazing novels but are terrible with computers, but your partner happens to be a computer whiz whose imaginative side could use stoking. Or you are a great artist and your partner is a fantastic businessperson. With this strategy, you can accomplish anything, because for this sign, two truly is more powerful than one.

With the right person, this Venus sign invests herself totally in the partnership—and needs a mate who does the same. In action and word, Venus in Libra demonstrates this through her attention to her partner's desires, careful strategizing, and follow-through in the relationship. Whether arranging a well-orchestrated moonlit walk on a beach, a thoughtful vacation itinerary, or a first-class seat at the symphony, Venus in Libra loves to please by creating blissful environments and experiences for her lover. The Libran Golden Rule is "give and you shall receive," so this exchange needs to be a two-way street. While it isn't necessary to rent the Taj Mahal for date night, a partner who isn't fifty-fifty and kicks back and allows Venus in Libra do all the work in the partnership will eventually disappoint this Venus sign.

THINK WITH YOUR VENUS MANTRA, VENUS IN LIBRA

I am blessed with dignity, charm, and grace, and so is my other half. As I embody mutual respect and empathy, I attract the same. As I value myself, others value me. I'm sensitive to our differences, and I don't need to change anyone to love them. I know our differences make our life and our love beautiful.

PEACE AT ALL COSTS

Because peace and balance are so important to this Venus sign, a troubled Venus in Libra can adopt a "peace at all costs" stance—leading her straight into the arms of conflict avoidance and thus unnecessary stress. Sure, undue conflict can cause stress, but an equal or greater mountain of stress is created when we avoid making waves. The biggest threat to

Venus in Libra's happiness is avoiding conflict, which, over time, can bring a great relationship to its knees.

In fact, the mere thought of conflict can make this Venus sign want to reach for a pint of her favorite ice cream or an ice-cold Guinness. Avoidance is Venus in Libra's shadow. In a misguided effort to avoid the stress of resolving the clashing mishmash of wants, needs, and desires that always exists when two or more people assemble in one place, Venus in Libra will go to great lengths to turn a blind eye and ignore the problem(s). As a result, when problems pile up and her partner becomes angry, instead of mobilizing her into practical action and response, those fiery hot emotions can have an opposite effect, causing this Venus to spin out, withdraw, or become even more dangerously passive.

Conflict is not the enemy, dear Venus in Libra; conflict is what happens when two universes collide. We may want to avoid stressful people and situations because they don't feel good to us, but when we have a partner, clearing the air restores sanity and peace to our lives. Conflict arises between two people when an old agreement needs to be renegotiated or a new one needs to be made. Conflict is an opportunity to air your feelings and bring peace back into your heart. Having a good fight and clearing the air can help move the sign of the Scales from unhappily together back to happy, peaceful, and in love. Remember, the point of conflict is to restore us to loving happiness.

Garden-variety negativity and stress do mar the silvery patina on this union, subtly diminishing its magical glow—which is why a partner who is coarse, crude, rude, or has violent tendencies is not for this Venus sign. But the avoidance of stressful subjects erodes it, too. Venus in Libra avoids vulgarity and stress, instinctually harmonizing with others, sometimes at the expense of her true feelings, needs, and desires—which causes stress! At this point, she may become deeply unhappy or believe her partner is unhappy with her. The reality is her unexpressed needs and desires have created an imbalance in the partnership, which this Venus must correct by bravely facing her unexpressed anger and wishes and sharing those with her partner. This is the strategy for keeping a relationship peaceful.

The good news is when it comes to conflict resolution, no one's better at it than you, Venus in Libra. Yet if you're having a hard time standing up for yourself or articulating your desires, needs, and passions, all that finessing, smoothing, and assuaging is no substitute for authentic self-expression. Perhaps assertiveness training is in order. Call on your counterpart—an Aries friend or therapist (or someone with Aries / Mars prominent in the birth chart)—to spark your courage and help you get what you need from love.

A MUTUAL LOVE

A Venus-in-Libra coupling is based on the old-fashioned concepts of civility and class. When successfully partnered, this Venus sign is the perfect picture of politeness and courtesy. No matter what's happening between the sheets or behind closed doors, Venus in Libra is not the type to willingly air her dirty laundry in public, out of consideration for her partner and the relationship itself. A code of conduct toward each other resembles that inner attitude. They must both agree to hold their relationship with the delicacy with which one might handle a crystal champagne flute, each dignifying the other with care and concern. *Both* partners must do this. Remember, a Venus-in-Libra relationship is not a one-way street.

For this to happen, one partner must never be placed either above or below the other. Ever heard the expression "He put her on such a high pedestal, even he couldn't reach her"? Venus in Libra has been guilty of putting her partner on a pedestal so high, she'd need a trampoline to reach the person. This may work for an Olympian god or goddess, but not for the mere mortal who forgets grocery lists and is late for dinner. Thus, the disappointment of seeing your beloved fall off the pedestal can be shocking, but frankly this can be avoided by simply paying attention to your own expectations and getting clear about whether it's someone else's responsibility to fulfill them for you. This will save you unwanted grief.

In any successful Venus-in-Libra union, equality and mutual respect must reign supreme. Then everything around the couple glides effortlessly into place. The ideal is a meeting of equals, of two people who value the other's individuality, intelligence, and freedom—including the freedom to choose to commit to and be with each other anew, every day. How do a truly noble prince and princess behave? With dignity and class. They take nothing, including each other, for granted. They don't put anyone on too high a pedestal or beneath them. The Venus-in-Libra relationship is civilized down to the bone.

Good graces go deeper than keeping up appearances; for Venus in Libra, they make a person profoundly trustworthy. When civility, courtesy, kindness, respect, and sensitivity are shared values in the relationship, trust comes easily. Then Venus in Libra can do the thing she loves most: enjoy her partnership.

YOUR EROTIC STRENGTH

Intelligence. Aphrodite was surely beautiful, but in her realm, great beauties were a dime a dozen. What separated her from the pack was her brainy intelligence, a unique combination of empathic understanding (she could make anyone feel seen and special) and sophisticated knowledge about the world that gave her a magnetic edge and drew lovers to her. So play up your smarts. Have intelligent conversations. Read books. Go to libraries (there's a Libra in every *library*). Revive old-school salons— cocktail-party-style gatherings where purveyors of taste and culture (intellectuals, artists, writers, and poets) would meet, discuss everything, and change the world with the chemistry sparked among them. Be the leader of sophistication and grace that you are.

IF YOU'RE IN LOVE WITH VENUS IN LIBRA...

Your Venus in Libra wants you to be her partner in life, every day and in every possible way. Business partners, friends, lovers, compatriots—she wants you in her corner and in her pocket, as this Venus sign prizes togetherness and loathes being alone. Rest assured that in deed and word, she has your happiness at heart, but for this love to work, it must be mutual. Be fifty-fifty and you're golden.

Venus in Libra is classically compatible with air signs (Gemini, Libra, Aquarius) and fire signs (Aries, Leo, Sagittarius), though she discovers an unparalleled equal in Scorpio, whose relationship orientation, love of commitment, and passion for romance and excitement mirror her own.

Venus in Scorpio
♏

Love people and stay beside them.

~JODIE FOSTER, VENUS IN SCORPIO

YOUR LOVE ELEMENT

Mysterious, mesmerizing, powerful—water can be as refreshing as a dip on a hot summer's day or as menacing as a tidal wave. Since water is serene and placid one day and unpredictable and deadly the next, it's no wonder some people have a fear of the sea's great depths or the hidden power of the tides. Water rules the irrational element of feeling—the invisible, tumultuous dimensions of our inner lives that we cannot see but only feel, and it's our most powerful feelings that drive us to create—and destroy. Water can be destructive, destroying villages in one lethal tsunami wave, or as focused as a hydroelectric dam, almighty and powerful. Water generates power, for good or ill. It all depends on how you use it.

Your Secret Desire

To be psychologically and emotionally naked in front of your intimates is about more than just baring your booty; it's about letting down your guard to reveal everything, including your deepest desires and fears. Through intimacy, you'll be profoundly seen and healed. Warning: baring all may cause you to honestly and directly ask for and try sexually taboo things that other signs only dream of!

Your Love Charms

- Your ability to remain relevant. Whether it's time for a dramatic new style or a relationship reinvention, you do this from the inside out.

- Your ability to change your look and appeal faster than you can say Lady Gaga. This is preceded by much soul-searching, but once you've made up your mind, you stop at nothing short of total reinvention.

- Your sexual magnetism. People find you irresistibly fascinating. Your vibration draws them in.

- Your kinky sense of humor. Your honest, deviant insights are so funny, you disarm foes and endear friends. If it's off-color or taboo, you delight in it.

- Your ruthless honesty. You can keep your heart under lock and key, but when stuff gets real and you care enough to share, you don't hold back. You courageously let others know what you're thinking and feeling.

- Your erotic intensity. Others may not know why you disarm them, but when they suspect their lives could be changed by you, they're right.

• Your fierce loyalty to those you love. When you're all in, you would die (and kill) for them. Equally, when they're out, they're dead to you.

YOUR LOVE GODDESS

It's hard for most of us to imagine life as a celebrity; their lives are too big, too mythic, to put ourselves in their shoes. Yet some actors have a hidden power, an ability to pull from a deeper place in themselves, evoking sides of our human experience that aren't always conscious. Jodie Foster's evocative and provocative performances reach those places inside of us. She is mesmerizing, drawing us toward her through fascination, an invisible transference of energy. Jodie shares her mysterious mesmerizing ability with others born under this Venus sign. Venus-in-Scorpio born enthrall those under their spell, conjuring up our hidden longing, our desire to be intimately known and seen. We may not understand why or how, but when we enter into a relationship with Venus in the sign of the conjurer, sorceress, and shaman, we are forever changed.

What accounts for this Venus's captivating mystery? Venus in Scorpio has animal magnetism, thanks to the two planetary rulers of Scorpio: Mars and Pluto. Mars is known for independent-mindedness, courage, and sexual autonomy, which, when combined with Pluto's penchant for honestly addressing social and sexual taboos, give this Venus the reputation for being the most intensely sexually erotic of all the Venus signs. When forces like these meet, relationships are passionate and demanding; Venus-in-Scorpio relationships are rarely neutral.

Venus in Scorpio may possess powerful sexual magnetism, but the attention this brings isn't always positive or wanted. This Venus may encounter the dark face of sexual desire and love: sexual abuse, abandonment, sexual addiction, obsessive attractions, and game playing. These negative situations provide the impetus to honestly confront, heal, and empower her relationship to her sexuality, self-esteem, and desires. A healthy Venus in Scorpio has an empowered relationship with her sensuality and sexuality.

Creative and financial partnerships are attractive to this Venus, as watery Scorpio likes to merge. Merging resources makes us more powerful than we'd be alone, which Scorpio loves, yet money can bind us to someone for life, so this Venus must be clear about people's motives for a merger. Emotional and material security is an alluring temptation, but this Venus values intimate growth above all else, and will extricate herself from a relationship that isn't serving that aim.

They say nothing lasts forever, yet Venus in Scorpio will tell you otherwise. This Venus is famous for holding on and never letting go. It must have been a Venus in Scorpio who wrote the vows "for better, for worse, for richer, for poorer, in sickness and in health, until death do us part." To keep the embers of love alive over time, she needs a committed partnership with someone for whom these vows aren't just spoken but viscerally felt in every cell of the body. This tenacity can be taken too far, though. Many a Venus in Scorpio has been known to be controlling, overly possessive, and manipulative toward partners—and when a relationship disappoints, this Venus can be unforgiving and vengeful. Care should be taken so her relationship life doesn't turn into a dark tale of obsession and mayhem.

This Venus sign seeks a strong emotional exchange of energy with her partner and needs a strong partner who won't be intimidated or dominated by her willful energy. Ultimately, Venus in Scorpio wants to be intimately known and understood by her partner. She wants to trust you with her entire self, including her shadow, wounds, secrets, strong sexuality, and eroticism. She wants the unshakable security of being intimately seen and met by a sexually empowered and psychologically self-aware equal. At her best, she is an emotionally courageous and fiercely supportive partner who will go to the ends of the earth for you. At her worst, she can be dark, demanding, and unforgiving. If you're ready for a life-changing relationship, say hello to the Scorpion Queen.

LOVE AND STAY BESIDE ME

Venus in Scorpio doesn't want a dull relationship; she craves ongoing excitement and heat in her partnerships, which is also probably why this Venus sign can be a sexual rogue who chooses short-term lovers over long-term commitment. Pop star and former first lady of France Carla Bruni is one example of a passionate Venus-in-Scorpio woman whose feminine sexual independence broke taboos, as she openly had many lovers. Yet nothing motivates Venus in Scorpio's spiritual growth like the juicy, exciting container of lifelong partnership.

Scorpio is the sign of lifelong intimacy. We can share snapshots of our lives with someone, but that's not the same as waking up next to someone day in and day out, sharing our innermost secrets, hurts, regrets, and dreams. Intimacy must be developed over time, in the willing bondage of a shared vow to love and stay beside each other.

What is so important about a committed vow, for Venus in Scorpio? There is a certain type of healing that can only happen through being fully seen in all our dark and wounded glory, by someone who can hold us through our pain, weakness, and darkness—someone who won't leave. Occasionally a really good therapist can see into the depths of our soul, but paying someone to be there for us isn't the same as having a partner who willingly embraces our dark and light sides, our whole selves in all their messy splendor, and loves us, and stays.

For Venus in Scorpio, committed love can be an indestructible cauldron in which to experience the trials and tribulations of life and provide opportunities for growth. When the waters of committed love get rocky, as they will for everyone, this Venus sign steps up to the plate. In fact, surviving a difficult experience together—the sickness or death of a loved one, a job loss, a marriage crisis—cements the bond of Venus-in-Scorpio love like nothing else, as the tough times have a way of bringing to the forefront this Venus's strengths: compassion, ruthless psychological honesty, tenacity, depth of feeling, courage, and loyalty.

The kinds of experiences that are available to us only through committed relationships—circumstances that test our love bond and force us into self-examination—are incredibly growth-inducing for this Venus. Surviving hardships like these together not only helps us appreciate the good times and gifts of life, it makes us whole, compassionate, and deep individuals. If a Venus-in-Scorpio relationship survives a life-altering ordeal, it always emerges from the embers stronger than before; but if it doesn't, then Venus in Scorpio learns precious transformative lessons, often surrounding loss and letting go.

Venus in Scorpio might enjoy ...
Firewalking, tantric eye gazing, burlesque dancing, designing and wearing Halloween costumes, mystical arts, Tarot, taboo conversations, psychoanalysis, erotic art, contact improvisational dance, shamanism, soul-claiming journeys, sexual therapy.

EROTIC CONJURER

You, Venus in Scorpio, are one seductively sexy creature, but due to the unconscious nature of your ruling planet, Pluto, many of you don't seem to realize this or tap its full potential. Do you know there are people who would do cartwheels to win your attention, to win a kiss from you? There are people who aspire to be your friend and your lover—probably both at once. They consider your sexuality smoldering and your vibe delightful. Can you even own such hotness? You must. You're one hot-blooded animal and far more thrillingly, erotically alive than the many vegetable life forms on this planet.

Your pleasure center is strong, but not all desires are to be followed. Every Venus sign needs to learn discernment. Scorpio delights in picking the forbidden fruits, gorgeous creatures who ooze sexual magnetism but are unavailable for a deeper relationship in some critical way. Addictive or unhealthy relationships can lead you to periods of celibacy in your life—necessary times for pulling your kundalini energy back in, purifying it, and reclaiming your sexuality and soul.

Kundalini—the life force energy coiled at the base of the spine, at the root chakra—is the erotic pulse of life for you. Through the course of Venus in Scorpio's healing in this lifetime, the kundalini serpent goddess awakens, traveling up the spine and increasing the sexual currents in the body. Developing more self-awareness and consciousness around your sexual energy gives you personal autonomy. You can connect with this precious energy in the presence of anyone or anything that turns you on. Scorpio is all about being intimately connected to that which charges you up with erotic intensity, fills your body with heat, and makes you feel alive. Whether it's a person or something else, when you feel that special charge, heed the call and gravitate in that direction. The kundalini has started to flow through your sacral center, the area above your pelvis known as the second chakra. This creative-sexual energy can be used for a variety of purposes, including sex, creativity, and magic and occult practices.

"Go where the energy is" is a foolproof strategy for getting Venus in Scorpio out of the dumps and into something alive and exciting. It's those people, ideas, and things that hold erotic life force for us that charge up our energetic bodies. So use it or lose it, baby! Just like life, the *erotic life* is meant for *living*.

Scorpio Alchemy

Venus in Scorpio is conversant in the sacred secrets of love alchemy, its means and its ways. The initiation into the Mystery School of Venus may be a poisonous or impossible relationship, but the way of transformation is through mining our relationship pain for gold. As such, Scorpio alchemy may be best explained through the tale of the Scorpion—a tale of three distinct evolutionary phases.

Scorpio is endowed with three animals: the snake, the eagle, and the phoenix, each representing a stage of personal evolution for this Venus sign. The Scorpio snake is always sexually magnetic, hypnotic, alluring, and powerful—until she strikes someone who crosses a boundary. The snake strikes when she senses deception or potential for hurt, be it real or imagined. The snake feeds on the unforgiving pain of our undigested wounds and our deepest fears. She stores that up, waiting until someone who triggers the perfect cocktail of abandonment fears and remembered pain gets close enough for her to strike.

When the reptilian mind—the part of our brain whose sole concern is our survival—kicks in, we convince ourselves that *it is their fault*. The snake is venomous and unforgiving. Relationships get really sticky at this point; it's hard to tell who is harming whom, but clearly people are hurting. The dynamic between the two people or the relationship itself needs to evolve—or the relationship will die.

Humility and honesty about our own pain is required to evolve into a higher life form: the eagle. We need to trade our emotional attachment for higher spiritual truths, our pride for an objective perspective. Capable of perceiving minute and accurate truths, but only from a distance, the eagle's penetrating vision is amazingly sharp and clear. We need to be the eagle, capable of both peering deep down inside ourselves and standing outside and apart from ourselves. The eagle sees and hears everything, but she flies above it all, attached to nothing. The eagle soars when we are capable of soaring to a higher truth about a person or situation with the help of someone with eagle-eyed vision, or through our own.

Having been liberated of our emotional attachments by the snake, and with the eagle's clear perspective and awareness, we next encounter the mythical phoenix. The Egyptians believed that every five hundred years, the phoenix bird renewed her quest for her true self by willingly dying. As a way for her worn-out habits, defenses, and patterns to die, she built a beautiful nest, sat in it, set it aflame, and afterward came back to life as a new bird, externally changed yet more like her essential self. Dying can be a literal physical process, but it can also be a psychic and soul process, one where we intentionally and willingly let go of a relationship, role, or identity because we must. A type of death—an ending—precedes every new beginning.

After she rose from the ashes, the phoenix was said to sing a song so truthful, so compassionate and beautiful, that the melody brought instant healing to anyone within earshot. Having tasted love and hate, death and life, tragedy and triumph, there was nothing left for her to do but let go, and share what she experienced. Just as a moving love song or heart-opening novel is always born of deep, transformative pain, when the phoenix sings her story of compassion and understanding, we hear it with our entire souls. Once healed, she heals others. The three-phase evolution of Venus in Scorpio is complete.

THINK WITH YOUR VENUS MANTRA, VENUS IN SCORPIO

I am erotically alive. I honor my emotional depth, sexual intensity, and honesty. I form empowering relationships based on mutual trust, which allows me to surrender my fears, let my guard down, and experience deep healing. When I encounter someone who does the same with me, this is the person I can trust with my soul.

INTIMACY AND HONESTY

Venus in Scorpio's relationship style is intense: she loves fiercely and devotedly and asks the same of you. Her loves and affections are intensely focused. Her need for passionate involvement in her relationships and creative life is like a coiled spring driving her inward into her own process. She is a ruthless explorer of relationships, and her desires, wants, and fears for her partnerships can consume her focus, thus earning her the stereotype of the obsessive "fatal attraction" lover. She feels things intensely; she loves and sometimes hates intensely, and perhaps is more honest about her dark feelings than most.

If you're wondering where all this erotic intensity comes from, Venus in Scorpio draws feminine power from the unconscious, that hidden storehouse of mysterious drives, memories, desires, and urges. Much of the time it's hard to know exactly what's in there, but we do know the unconscious holds a lot of powerful energy, which explains the strong charge other people feel when in the presence of this Venus sign. Just as Venus in Scorpio draws energy from this mysterious, powerful source, she is also magnetized toward it in others. One way to exchange this energy is through sex. Mystics believe sex transmits energy. Perhaps fluids and scents also encapsulate memories, desires, secrets, and life force, and this co-mingling nurtures her erotically, viscerally, and emotionally.

Another way to exchange and circulate this energy is through honest sharing. The power of honest, emotional sharing should not be underestimated for this Venus. Polls have shown that many spouses and partners would consider an emotional affair a greater betrayal than "just sex." Unadulterated emotional bonding can be hotter than sex. Likewise, when we're not being truthful with our partners about our emotions, or we're hiding something from ourselves, we can lose our libido or develop sexual problems. The mind can hide the truth, but the body can't.

To seduce this Venus sign, bring your passionate intensity, depth, and ability to bond emotionally—that's foreplay to her. Venus in Scorpio delights in both sensually and psychologically unwrapping things—taking it all off and then honestly breaking it down. So don't give away your pretty lingerie. To ignite the smoldering embers of a mediocre or nonexistent sex life, put on your best lingerie and then tell the truth. Undress each other with emotional honesty.

Unconscious Saboteur

Erotica writer Anaïs Nin once said, "We see others as we are, not who they are." This accurately sums up so many of our Venus/relationship problems!

There's always much more to this Venus sign than meets the eye, and since so much is going on beneath the surface, during relationship troubles it can be helpful for Venus in Scorpio to look at two unconscious archetypes: the saboteur and the shadow. The saboteur is the archetype made up of the fears and insecurities that block our power. When we act out of fear, we act against our true desires and sabotage our chances at happiness. The shadow is a matrix of qualities we dislike in others; we attract shadowy people to alert us to what we've disowned or rejected or haven't developed in ourselves. The following exercise, "Identify Your Saboteur," is excerpted from my book *A Love Alchemist's Notebook*.

1. What fears do I give authority to in my life? Name three.

2. What emotional and situational triggers lead me into pointless, repetitive, or self-destructive behavior?

3. Can I see the role of my saboteur with a person I still haven't forgiven or in a relationship I haven't been able to move on from?

Sometimes our saboteur or shadow shows up as a person who appears intent on undermining us. If you're having this experience, consider that this person might be a reflection of what you've rejected in yourself—your fears and low self-esteem. These archetypes undermine us when they remain unconscious, but when we become conscious of them, we are empowered. We no longer make the same old mistakes.

SHADOWS AND SHAMANS

They say "don't judge a book by its cover," and this is wise advice for those who love a Venus in Scorpio. The inner life of someone with this Venus is complex and often hidden, at least initially. It's worth taking the time to get to know this Venus sign.

Jealousy, obsession, unforgivingness, and power struggles are just some of the garden-variety relationship issues for those with Venus in Scorpio. With a rap sheet like that, it's not hard to understand why ancient astrologers considered Venus to be "in detriment" in Scorpio. This is the only zodiac sign whose symbol carries a weapon—a self-protective stinger—and she carries this for a reason. In the karmic past, she has been hurt, lied to, betrayed. Today, this Venus needs to make peace with the relationship dynamics that have damaged her trust in the past and use that wisdom as insurance against the future while not creating defenses against loving others. She has the resources to do this, as she is penetratingly insightful and psychologically honest and has spiritual powers rivaling any other Venus sign.

Venus in Scorpio has a sixth sense for secrets. This Venus may suspect secret liaisons or question another's love for her. She will know when someone is not being truthful or not telling her the whole story. In her unyielding desire to get to the bottom of things, to strip falsity and pretense bare, Venus in Scorpio can be so single-pointed on a subject that she can push a point to the edge of exhaustion and a relationship to the brink of breaking. Sometimes this Venus sign needs to do something not "deep," like go to a movie, read a book, or just take a walk. This calming strategy can be a relationship saver during times of crisis.

Venus in Scorpio can be demanding, especially if she's not feeling valued by her partner. She gives so much of herself to a relationship, financially, spiritually, and emotionally, and while she doesn't need her efforts to be reciprocated tit for tat, she does need to feel that they are appreciated. If she isn't feeling valued, her Scorpion stinger comes out, and she may lash out in anger, or worse, silently nurse her bitterness.

In a relationship, she can stubbornly hang on to built-up grievances, but sometimes the hard but right thing to do is to let go. She can find it hard to forgive people who have hurt her. This Venus has a shaman's ability to transmute energy. Psychological work transforms negative energy. Magical rituals, prayers of release, and forgiveness can also discharge emotional energy from the body.

If this Venus sign is obsessed with a partner or is on the verge of being called paranoid by her friends because she can't let go of a suspicion, her insecurity may be the culprit. She may truly be afraid of betrayal, loss, or abandonment to such an extent that she focuses all of her energy on her partner by demanding honesty, attention, or commitment. Paradoxically, by clinging even harder to the symbolic significance and meaning of a partner or relationship, she is forced to ruthlessly and sometimes painfully face her own dependencies, fears, and illusions—so she can let them go. Venus in Scorpio is learning that true security can only come from within herself. She attains the inner security she craves by compassionately loving and transmuting what's hardest in herself to love: her own pain. When she has done this, she is liberated to conjure a new kind of love, one where the dappled interplay of light and dark enriches her soul.

YOUR EROTIC STRENGTH

Desire. Desire is as natural to humankind as fire and water, and just as powerful. In the sacred dance of Shakti and Shiva, desire creates and destroys the entire world! You may know the depths of your own desire, or just a hint of it. Look at everything you can do with your desire, and the world becomes an enchanting place. Play with your desire. Eros is a big flirt! With your Venus in Scorpio, you love to be played with, tempted, and teased. Honor your desire as sacred; your most sacred desires motivate true happiness. Look underneath your desires; not all that glitters is gold. Sometimes more precious desires are revealed after peeling back false desires. Respect your desire; if it is too intense, desire is capable of burning the things and people you care about. Use your desire; mold, shape, and manifest your dreams with the fire of your passions. Accept your desires; release any body or sexual shame you have by accepting it. Take your desire as you would a lover; harness the power of desire, have your way with it, and then be willing to be transformed by it.

IF YOU'RE IN LOVE WITH VENUS IN SCORPIO...

Your Venus in Scorpio mesmerizes you with her subtle power, mystery, and depth of understanding. She demands a lot from herself and gives much to you, so don't let the contributions she makes to your life go unacknowledged or she'll be unhappy. Above all, this Venus sign wants an emotionally supportive, erotically exciting, and honest relationship with you. In return, she offers you her unwavering commitment, perceptiveness, and passion—the love of a lifetime.

Venus in Scorpio is classically compatible with water signs (Cancer, Scorpio, Pisces) and earth signs (Taurus, Virgo, Capricorn), though she also finds that Libra's tendency toward impartiality brings objectivity to her emotional nature.

Venus in Sagittarius

♐

The easiest kind of relationship for me is with ten thousand people.
The hardest is with one.

~JOAN BAEZ, VENUS IN SAGITTARIUS

YOUR LOVE ELEMENT

Expansive, passionate, inspired—fire is the alpha and omega element. Fire's discovery introduced new potentials to reach beyond what humans thought was possible. Fire ignites the spark of possibility that exists inside each and every one of us, inspiring hunger for passion and new experiences. Just observe how fire, fueled by oxygen, quickly covers a lot of ground. Fire enthusiastically fans the flames of our passion to explore, to know and discover more. Once it gets going, fire is tireless and nearly unstoppable, appearing to survive on sheer enthusiasm alone. Fire has no regrets. Unencumbered by the past, fire moves forward toward ever-greater potentials. Anything's possible with fire.

YOUR SECRET DESIRE

You want to grow with a partner, which probably means you want to go somewhere together, too. Your love activities include, but are not limited to, erotic explorations, mystical meanderings, and mutual explorations of mind, body, and spirit. While you will have out-of-body oohs, ahs, and "aha!" experiences with a variety of partners, the one for you eternally delights in your starry-eyed wonder.

YOUR LOVE CHARMS

- Your ability to throw caution to the wind in the name of a really good time, a big adventure, or a promising new love affair.

- You call it like you see it. Dishonesty bothers you, though the truth is relative, isn't it?

- Your "willing to relocate" love clause. You can travel far and wide to visit the Seven Wonders of the World, and on your way, you discover the Eighth: love.

- An afternoon drive, a lazy Saturday, a weekend trip— you've got a talent for making any event, no matter how mundane, into a grand adventure.

- You're worldly. You've got instant chemistry with people from all walks of life. The stranger, the better; you always find something to groove on, together.

- You're an experientialist at heart. You attract diverse people with exotic interests and ideas because they widen and enrich your life journey.

- Your unparalleled appetite for fun. You suck the marrow from the bone and drink nectar from the chalice of the gods. This makes you a pleasure to know!

YOUR LOVE GODDESS

Tina Turner (b. 1939) is known as the Queen of Rock 'n' Roll. Born of African American, European, and Native American (Cherokee and Navajo) descent, Tina is a rock 'n' roll royal with a little piece of every woman contained therein. In terms of cultural representation alone, Tina embodies the colorful gypsy archetype of Sagittarius, a sign that loves to roam freely across cultural divides. During performances, Tina's positivity, enthusiasm, and high energy (Venus in Sagittarius strengths) are irrepressible, garnering attention and admiration from peers and fans. Her career appears to be unstoppable, too. Tina created a solo career in which she soared to even more astounding levels of success, but not before she earned her freedom.

Tina Turner, the irrepressible performer, was once an abused woman. She finally extricated herself from Ike Turner's grip after enduring sixteen years of abuse and controlling behavior. Tina credits spirituality, specifically Buddhism and chanting, for helping her gather the strength to walk away from her husband. This Venus enjoys finding a philosophy, system, or meaningful life pattern that fits her values: to connect to and experience one's own existence as infinitely greater than one's small self. Sagittarius is also a sign that learns best through firsthand experience. Rather than sign up for a relationship workshop or read about love in books, Sagittarius dives right in. Sagittarius knows life is a teacher and there are no shortcuts for the education of living and learning. If it's sometimes messy, chaotic, and painful—that's a face of love, too.

Venus in Sagittarius can be high-minded and idealistic, inclined to avoid the human stuff that comes with love. From questions of compromise to whose turn is it to wash the laundry to heartbreak, love is always a gamble. There's no guarantee that the same partner who loves us today won't hurt us tomorrow. As a fire sign ruled by Jupiter, the planet of expansion and opportunity, Venus in Sagittarius motivates and is motivated by growth in relationships. This sign possesses faith that things will work out just fine, and it usually does, because even when it doesn't, she can see the silver lining of the cloud. This Venus takes a philosophical approach toward disappointment. When she works out the higher math, she understands the lessons learned and spiritual gains made, figuring that if falling in love is a gamble, the bigger loss is walking away without ever having fallen. A hopeless romantic, this Venus is willing to risk everything for love.

Ever the philosophical optimist, she learns from everyone and everything, and has a rollicking good time doing so. Sagittarius's glyph is a centaur, half horse and half man. Venus in Sagittarius is a true seeker who loves connecting with other like-minded philosophers and gypsies, while her animal nature simply wants to sing, drink, and be merry. Whether she's chasing her lover through the forest like a nymph or philosophizing about the meaning of the cosmos, her appetites are pagan, intellectual, and experiential. Open to the adventure inherent in each moment, this Venus sign is one of the most exciting, adventurous, optimistic, and enthusiastic companions around.

Venus in Sagittarius needs to keep growing in and through her relationships. Socializing, traveling, and engaging with a wide variety of people are some of this sign's favorite things to do; but when it comes to a committed relationship, one that will last beyond a string of weekends, the spark of ongoing growth must be present. In a relationship, she needs to feel like she and her partner are growing and going somewhere together, for this Venus lives for the twinkle of possibility. Possibility, which implies freedom, is like air for her, and without freedom, she finds it impossible to breathe.

Through the ordeals of her marriage to Ike, Tina Turner did what every Venus in Sagittarius knows how to do: turn a seemingly impossible, oppressive situation into "I'm possible." Through trials of faith and crises of self-worth, the sign of Sagittarius offers Venus true self-understanding and wisdom. For her optimism and spiritual resiliency, and for mastering the number-one lesson we all need to learn to be a goddess—radical self-love—may Tina's transformational journey inspire you.

APPETITE FOR ADVENTURE

Sagittarius is the sign of possibility, and anything's possible for this Venus. She lives to expand her mind and her world, and to keep on expanding into ever-greater possibilities. She does this by continually exposing herself to diverse experiences, ideas, places, and people. This applies particularly to love. In the world according to Venus in Sagittarius, there are as many possibilities to be had through partnering as there are stars hanging in the heavens. In her eyes, love is like the night sky. She sees how vast, limitless, and covered with stars it is. It's hard for her not to imagine taking a trip to Jupiter—but not before getting lost in a comet's tail on the way to Mars. Itineraries change, reroutes happen. She is searching for someone who hangs the Moon for her, over and over and over again.

So what's a Venus with an appetite for adventure to do but dive right in? A typical astrologer will say your penchant for exploration, growth, freedom, and personal expansion aligns your Venus sign with the popular archetypes of the bachelor or bachelorette. Being footloose and fancy-free may indeed feel more right for you than settling down, and there's nothing wrong with not settling down with one person—though society may tell you otherwise. The social and familial pressure to get married and have 2.5 kids can go through the roof, yet we know that's no formula for success. Just ask any Venus in Sagittarius who married too soon, before she got to know herself, how well that worked out. Accumulating relationship experience and getting a life of one's own are prerequisites for every person who wants to enter a relationship whole, instead of half. Having a few different types of partners before committing to a lifelong love is the right strategy for you.

Venus in Sagittarius might enjoy...

Philosophical discussions, spiritual teachings, gurus, books, metaphysical mixers, travel, a trip around the world, classes and learning, culture shock, a social tribe, sporting events, plus tribal art, clothes, music, and gifts from different cultures.

EXOTIC ROMANTIC

The fabric of your ideal Venusian existence resembles Aladdin's magic carpet: you may be the one happily flying off to Marrakesh at a moment's notice or taking a spontaneous trip for mango lassi in the next town over. When you catch wind of an exotic adventure or a person offering discovery and intrigue, you're all over it, because for zealous Venus in Sagittarius, the bliss of being made brand-new again is forever and always just one more adventure, plane ride, spiritual retreat, guru—and, most especially, romantic encounter—away.

Exotic encounters with unusual people, places, ideas, and philosophies make up the core of your romantic happiness. The definition of the word *exotic* is essentially "different," so extraordinary encounters with people who are in any way different are fun for you. They don't have to be from Timbuktu or the lost city of Atlantis; they may simply not have the same cultural or geographical background as you. In fact, encounters with people who are most different from you will likely develop into the most profound relationships you have.

Sometimes the only way to have your mind blown wide open and your senses shocked into delight is by embracing something (perhaps someone) different from you. You may be delighted to discover that culture shock pleasurably shakes things up in your world and actually calms you down, relaxes you, and brings you beautiful bliss. Shocks to your pleasure sensibilities reward you with unshakable internal peace—hence your reputation as an exotic romantic. What better way to be delightfully stimulated than by love?

FREEDOM LOVER

When it comes to pursuits of pleasure, Sagittarius's hedonistic appetite earns the motto "go big or go home." You may fall in love with a place, only to realize that to have the total experience, you need to immerse yourself in everything about it. You may fall in love with a philosophy, or a person, and find yourself moving quickly, jumping in feet first, wanting to learn everything about them. When Venus in Sagittarius falls for a place, idea, or person, she wants the full monty.

You are voted "Most Likely to Jump Right into Love" because love is growth-inducing, which revs you up to no end. You're also wary of anyone who limits your freedom—hence this sign's reputation as the perpetual bachelor or bachelorette. Instead of being a dire prediction about your love life, this is a positive prophecy on how to go about getting who and what you most desire. Someone you can grow with is great, sure; but someone invested in their own self-actualization, and who enthusiastically and wholeheartedly supports yours, is the one you can get behind and support and love. You need this in a partner, because you need the same for you. Anyone who truly loves you will honor your need for freedom to develop yourself and grow. Know that committed love and freedom are not mutually exclusive, and if you have a buried belief that they are, you will attract relationships that always end up limiting you in some way.

If you become restless from staying in one place for too long or you get bored in a relationship, it could be because the person or place is not intellectually or philosophically stimulating enough for you. Likewise, some Venus-in-Sagittarius born are philosopher-teacher types who like to be admired and esteemed by their lovers for their wisdom and knowledge. This is similar to a guru and her student; when the student has graduated and learned all she can, the teacher moves on. Fire Venus signs want enthusiasm and appreciation from their partners, and when they don't get it, they may go looking elsewhere.

Your soulmates may not hold the same exact beliefs or ideologies as you, but they value exploration and growth; they want to push the boundaries of the known world and drink life's sweet ambrosia out there—together, with you.

Your partner may be from a different culture or have a different background or religion. A Republican dating a Democrat may be a recipe for crazy to some, but for you this type of relationship could provide just the right amount of stimulation and culture shock, leading you to consider new realities and perspectives. Sagittarius can be quite evangelical about what she believes is right, but Venus is a lover of paradox: she knows there are different strokes for different folks. She advises: don't push someone away because of their differences; draw them closer and endeavor to understand and learn from them. Enjoy having your mind blown.

THINK WITH YOUR VENUS MANTRA, VENUS IN SAGITTARIUS

I honor my need for spontaneity and sensual exploration in relationships. Every day is a new opportunity to try, taste, and experience something radically different from the day before. I revel in the dazzling perspectives and possibilities that all of my partnerships offer me. I know all things are possible with love.

YOU SEXY BEAST

Generally, Venus in Sagittarius has a robust sexual appetite. Your Venus sign is the centaur: half man, half beast. After a day of walking around on two legs, you need to get down on all fours and feed your bestial nature. You can do this through sex, through sports, or through dancing and getting into your body. If sporting around sounds too pedestrian to the bookworms of your sign, the gist is: it's good for you to run with the wolves, to move, to make love, and to dance, because this helps you get into your body senses. Your body wants you to joyously follow your animal hungers—physical, sensual, and sexual. You're a natural at going with what feels right; you're vibrant and seductive when you just go with what you feel in the moment.

Your favorite forms of foreplay are more active than not and may involve wrestling and games like hide and seek. You can afford to be forthright about setting the stage for being pleasing and being pleased. Candlelight may set the mood, for example, but so too might an impromptu reading of the *Arabian Nights* or getting caught in a downpour while hiking. Frolicking in the forest, sex in exotic locales, lovemaking in wide-open fields (or anywhere in nature)—all such sensual explorations are especially stimulating for you. Try it. You may find this to be truly thrilling even if the rest of your birth chart is shy or timid. For inspiration, remember that Venus is a seductive love huntress, and Sagittarius a hunter…you can see where this is going. Free-thinking, free-spirited, up for anything, and sexually generous—all these qualities make you an exciting sexual partner.

Claiming a robust sexual appetite serves a deeper purpose than merely having fun; it's about joyously, shamelessly inhabiting your body and appetites. And, according to Venus-in-Sagittarius Alyssa Milano, sex is good for the health: "I feel a lot healthier when I'm having sex. I feel jitters when I wake up in the morning. I take vitamins, I work out every day. When I'm having sex I don't have that."

Your Venus sign lives to explore and experience all the intrigues of sexual delight, which means partners with sexual inhibitions and hang-ups only hold up your sensual experimentation and explorations. Karmically, or earlier in this life, you may have experienced shame around your sexual appetites. Now it's time to throw sensual caution and inhibition to the wind. Sexually generous and enthusiastic, you will want to be with a sexual partner of like mind.

DESTINATION WANDERLUST

Generally, Venus-in-Sagittarius people have an abiding appreciation for travel, and so have been known to have a lover in each port of call. A few nights spent together on a tropical island doesn't necessarily mean Venus in Sagittarius wants a committed relationship, yet sometimes before she realizes it, she's in one. When the other person starts planning their weekends around her, and then their vacations, this Venus can find herself quite suddenly—and seemingly without meaning to—in a relationship. Venus in Sagittarius was simply on holiday!

If this Venus is single, her sheer enthusiasm for a new love affair can convince the other person it's going somewhere. Is it? This is where it's helpful to pull back your arrow, Archer, and clarify your aim. You can get lots of stamps in your love passport, and there's no shame in that, but just practice full disclosure. Be upfront about remaining unattached, because it's better for your karma, and the other person's. Even if you don't give a whit about karma, be upfront, if for no other reason than you'll save energy on avoiding their phone calls, texts, and e-mails, and they'll save money on Kleenex. As a consenting adult, you can and should go about your business guilt-free.

Whether a sexual adventure or a blissful marriage, partnerships are meant to leave you feeling expanded, happy, and better about yourself. In love, you can cover vast distances and have epic experiences together. This is a grand strategy for nurturing your committed relationship. In fact, you don't need to always travel together, as traveling apart is growth-inducing, too. A weekend rendezvous is fun, but it takes a special person to inspire love for a lifetime. Your relationship should have an "us" consciousness that embodies the idea that we can both grow together—and we can go places together, too. A spirit of adventure, of self-actualization and mutual freedom, keeps your relationship fresh.

A Venus in Sag's appetite for adventure may be unparalleled, but the day-to-day experience of a relationship isn't always the grand adventure she wants it to be, with bills to pay, mouths to feed, and differences to negotiate. Sagittarius's ruling planet is

Jupiter, and in myth, King Jupiter restlessly searched for greener pastures, often leaving the humdrum routine work of the relationship (taking out the trash, walking the dog, raising the children) to his wife, Hera, who quickly grew to resent him. To make a partnership work, there must be a balance and respect for both heaven and earth—the extraordinary potentials and possibilities inherent to the relationship and the shared ordinary obligations of it. We can grow and go places together, but we still need to take out the trash!

Heaven and earth can be yours, Venus in Sagittarius. With the right person, you won't be settling for less than you deserve, nor will you be giving up your freedom to keep growing and learning. With the right partner, you will feel confident, expansive, and more capable as an individual—all the time. When you've got all this, you've hit the bull's-eye, Archer. Because unlike a weekend fling, Planet Bliss (Venus) has no expiration date and is not place-specific. Planet Bliss is a perpetual state of being blissed out, blessed, and loved for as long as time allows.

THE ULTIMATE ADVENTURE

Genuine, honest, spontaneous, and fun-loving, Venus in Sagittarius is a joy to be around. This Venus promises her lovers that every day is an adventure to be had, or at least holds the potential to be. But adventure for strictly adventure's sake isn't Sag's style. There is a transpersonal bent to Venus in Sagittarius, more so than people realize. Venus in Sagittarius wants an Ultimate Adventure, one much more valuable than exercises and experiments in making life exciting. The ultimate experience Sagittarius seeks is that of Truth.

Philosophers, scholars, monks, travelers, and wanderers all seek truth in the form of an understandable system, a way of relating the personal to the universal. Truth is a way of connecting our life experience to a cosmic one. Venus in Sagittarius wants to connect her personal experience to something larger than herself. How do we experience this alignment of our personal vision with a grander one? We know where we won't find it. Truth probably won't be found by sitting at a desk of an accounting firm, pursuing a safe, easy, and complacent life, nor by staying in your birth town your whole life. We taste truth through experience, the kind of experience that throws us out of our comfort zone, because Truth with a capital "T" is life-changing and mind-blowing.

The poetry of Rumi can shatter us in one verse: "Your task is not to seek for love, but merely to seek and find all the barriers within yourself that you have built against it." What kind of experiences did this soul have in order to arrive at such a place of wise understanding? To have these types of realizations, we must grow familiar with the uncomfortable feeling of having our comfort zones pushed, our innermost thoughts and cherished ideas questioned and expanded. The shock of experiencing another culture, the titillation of good-natured philosophical debates, and the revelations of spiritual exploration are all vehicles for truth to enter.

Like the expansive rings of Jupiter spreading outward into the Milky Way, taking up ever more space, you can accompany Venus in Sagittarius on the Ultimate Adventure, but don't expect her to fully arrive, or be satisfied. Her hunger propels her ever onward, ever outward. After all, it was Rumi who also said, "Two there are who are never satisfied—the lover of the world and the lover of knowledge." Venus in Sagittarius existentially hungers for more, and if you're up for an ultimate adventure, hop onto her spaceship. There's no better partner.

YOUR EROTIC STRENGTH

Enthusiasm. You move through the universe as though it were an incomplete game of *Mad Libs*, marveling at all the playful combinations you discover along the way. Entertaining the big questions in life, your mind opens ever wider, and you discover even more scenarios to entertain and share, while never losing your perspective or your sense of humor. Your erotic enthusiasm is contagious and your conviction is convincing; when you are turned on by an idea, place, or person, we want to follow you and get lost in your comet tail. You have little time for bleak world-weariness but all the time in the world for a quick pick-me-up or any opportunity to look at the world from a different, expansive point of view. You'd rather enjoy the view and look for the positive than gripe about something. And because you insist on looking for the silver lining, you always find it.

IF YOU'RE IN LOVE WITH
VENUS IN SAGITTARIUS...

Your Venus in Sagittarius promises you that life with her will be a colorful adventure, and she delivers by supplying mind-expanding conversations, experiences, and hijinks. She seeks an able co-pilot who wants to cross spiritual borders and cultural boundaries together. A true student of life who wants to share the wisdom she has acquired, Venus in Sagittarius likes to be esteemed for her knowledge, so in a philosophical pinch, admiration will get you everywhere.

Venus in Sagittarius is classically compatible with fire signs (Aries, Leo, Sagittarius) and air signs (Gemini, Libra, Aquarius) but gets along peachy with wise, metaphysical Pisces, who leans in the same mystical directions as she—and Sagittarius's impulsivity could be mellowed by Pisces' emotional side.

Venus in Capricorn
♑

He's a homebody, I have my freedom. He likes to stay at home
and he doesn't want me in his face all the time
and I don't want to be in it, so it works …
we respect each other's space and we like each other a lot.

~DOLLY PARTON, VENUS IN CAPRICORN

YOUR LOVE ELEMENT

Stable, sensual, sensible—earth has nothing to prove. Mother Earth simply is. In the infinite wisdom of enduring earth, she knows she has all the time in the world. Fads come and go; people are born and they die; wars happen, as do times of peace. Yet earth remains, silent and fecund, doing her job. A patient timekeeper, earth waits. Earth knows that this too will pass, and time heals all wounds. Those who learn to respect, use, and conserve her resources prosper. Occasionally she grumbles and quakes, reminding us that human life can be turned to rubble in an instant, so we learn to respect the gravitas and laws of earth, honoring the precarious dependence we have upon her. She is the earth who has been here before us and who will outlast us. Underneath her cool and calm exterior, molten hot lava flows.

YOUR SECRET DESIRE

To be with someone who is as capable, loyal, and self-sufficient as you are. This cool realism can make you seem detached or unavailable to some, but those are the wrong people for you anyhow. You have a sixth sense for those who possess the seed of inner authority, maturity, humor, and possibly great ambition, and you gravitate toward those people. Your love advertisement for a grown-up partnership reads: "Mama's boys and dependents need not apply."

YOUR LOVE CHARMS

- You keep it real. Because you value realism and maturity in all your relationships, you don't put on airs by pretending to be someone you're not.

- You know slower is better. It takes time and patience to get to know a person, and your thoughtful, take-it-slow pace allows us to trust you.

- Maturity and wisdom look good on you. Maturity isn't always measured in years. No matter your age, you're wise beyond your years.

- You're impressive. In words, speech, and style, you leave an indelible impression on us. Whether or not you want to be, you're memorable.

- Your thoughtful consideration. In these "love 'em and leave 'em" times, your astute care doesn't go unnoticed.

You take care to notice and acknowledge what many don't, earning you a permanent place in our hearts.

- You're committed. When you sign your name on the dotted line, you mean business. You believe that how you treat others comes back to you, and you're committed to do right by others.

- You age backwards. For you, wrinkles are beauty marks in disguise. Your friendly relationship with the planet of time, Saturn (Capricorn's planet), means that the older you get, the more confident you feel about yourself.

YOUR LOVE GODDESS

Every Venus sign needs a capable heroine, an unparalleled example of the magical powers of Venus, and yours is embodied by the talented, accomplished literary visionary Virginia Woolf (1882–1941). In the Victorian household that Virginia called home, the oppressive atmosphere was tighter than a corset in one-hundred-degree heat. Despite the social and familial conventions and the stifling gender oppressions that were at the heart of Victorian society, Virginia found her voice, and in her voice, her authority. Like Virginia, Venus-in-Capricorn born want to be taken seriously, so they are blessed with grit, the strength of character to make things happen, and, if so inclined, the artistic aptitude to create something enduring in the process.

But first this Venus may have to survive intolerable conditions. Any planet in the wintry sign of Capricorn earns merit badges for its ability to endure early hardships and obstacles; that's how this Venus sign learns to be self-reliant and stand on her own two feet. Venus in Capricorn's mother figure is often overly rigid, distant, or even altogether absent. At age thirteen,

Virginia's mother died, and that's when signs of Virginia's life-long mental instability first appeared. She was thought to have what is now known as bipolar disorder, with episodes of crippling depression followed by manic highs of elation and grandeur. Through loss and limitation, she learned the lessons of independence and autonomy, which are so important to this Venus sign; Virginia had to learn to take care of herself.

Those with Venus in Capricorn yearn to make their mark and leave evidence of their existence. Writing gave Virginia a private place to explore her feelings, thoughts, and experiences in depth and without risk of shame, rejection, or judgment; it gave Virginia the authority to trust her own responses. Journaling one's innermost thoughts was surely a Venus-in-Capricorn invention, as this Venus sign enjoys the privacy and solitude necessary to reach her own conclusions about life.

This Venus sign often enjoys structured personal free time or the solitude of perfecting an art form. As Virginia recorded her responses to the world around her, her personal diaries shaped a movement in literature—what Virginia herself called "the inner narrative," a doorway into her rich inner world. In her writings, Virginia explored outdated social conventions that limited her: the hypocrisy of the times, biological traps, gender roles, vanities, social expectations, and peacocking, or dressing for attention. Venus in Capricorn wryly observes social vanities as they are, then takes a capricious joy in disassembling them. Capricorn has a reputation for being overly serious, but when expressing through Venus, this sign has a wicked fun sense of humor.

This Venus sign craves solitude, so she chooses relationships where two lovers can be happy together as well as apart. Being with a partner who supports her need for creative solitude and autonomy is imperative for Venus in Capricorn. Virginia married Leonard Woolf, who supported her creative authority wholeheartedly by collaborating with her on books and creating a printing press together. Even though Virginia died prematurely at age fifty-nine, their lifelong marriage brought her great happiness. Virginia wrote in her diary: "Love-making— after twenty-five years, can't bear to be separate…you see it is enormous pleasure being wanted: a wife. And our marriage so complete."

Venus is how we trust and connect with others; in Capricorn, Venus needs someone reliable, respectable, and supportive. Being with partners she can count on gives her the rock-solid foundation she needs to self-actualize and bloom. Once in a committed partnership, Venus in Capricorn must meet relationship dynamics as they are, not the sugar-coated version we often pretend them to be. In response to a past relationship that failed due to the immaturity of one or both partners, she is ready today to build a relationship that goes the distance, with all the work that's implied.

Relationships are mundane and unexciting at times—the opposite of the glamour romances that Hollywood sells. But this Venus sign wouldn't be happy with anything less than real love. Integrity, reliability, maturity, wisdom…these aren't fleeting feelings but character traits she trusts and can count on as reliably as the sunrise and sunset. And when she earns her own self-respect and integrity, she begins to age backwards. Her wise, sage eyes sparkle. She's at home within herself.

SERIOUS FUN

Venus generally likes to be around other people; her sign describes our social nature. Unlike some other Venus signs, Venus in Capricorn does not fear or dread being alone—not at all! She needs regular periods of alone time, as solitude helps her to relax and recover her peace of mind and sanity.

This Venus sign embodies the archetype of the hermit. If that sounds a bit unglamorous, think again! Tyra Banks and Scarlett Johansson are both Venus-in-Capricorn babes. Venus-in-Capricorn born are industrious and need alone time to accomplish some form of satisfying activity or hobby that brings them happiness (no one accomplishes greatness if they're too busy cavorting to sit down and focus). As other Venus signs flit about looking for a new someone or something that suits their fancy, Venus in Capricorn knuckles down. She gets intimate with an art, craft, or hobby; she explores more deeply her love for genealogy, scrapbooking, dance, or architectural design. In the pursuit of pleasure, she can find some serious fun.

Fun as an accomplishment—fun as serious? It's not an oxymoron. Alone time allows this Venus to descend into the inner well of experience, to explore the touchstone within. As sense impressions bubble up and take shape, she discovers a world of imagination; and as an earthy Venus sign with gravitas, she will leave tangible evidence of her creative process or inner life in a substantial art form or her career. Capricorn is here to make something happen.

The sign of Capricorn offers impressive *authority* to the planet occupying it. Many authors have Venus in Capricorn, including Toni Morrison, Louisa May Alcott, and Robert Bly. What is authorship if not giving authority to our perceptions, thoughts, ideas, and impressions? Notably, this Venus sign likes to have her contributions recognized, as Capricorn lives to make a contribution to society, to stand up and be noticed for her achievements. Venus in Capricorn is blessed with the perseverance and commitment to do exactly that. With her willingness to work, to put in the hours and the effort, patient craftsmanship is a pleasure. Her interests may start out as a private affair, but over time, she wants to share them with others and eventually have her name recognized by her community. This Venus in the sign of authorship was born to make her mark.

Likewise, this Venus sign's relationship life risks revolving around professional roles and home and family obligations to the exclusion of playful downtime. Factoring play dates into the schedule can keep the relationship fresh and alive.

Venus in Capricorn might enjoy ...
Power walks, power breakfasts, hiking, trekking, backpacking, mountain retreats, writing and reading, cold and rainy days, wintertime, Christmas, genealogical studies, family get-togethers, professional attire, antiques, classic movies and clothing styles.

LIBERATED PLEASURES
Whether subliminal or blatant, Venus in Capricorn is so sensitive to familial and social pressures—the "shoulds" and "should nots"—that the open and easy lightness of Venus can become cautiously inhibited and restrained by Capricorn correctness. What happens when a woman's natural sensual and social instincts are inhibited? In mild doses, people-pleasing and shyness ensue. At worst, she suffers low confidence in her body image and sexuality.

If a Venus in Capricorn restrains herself socially or sexually, as though consulting an inner rulebook, it is a matter of conditioning and insecurities that she needs to work through and not at all a statement about her essential self. In some families, spoken or unspoken rules in the house around social appropriateness create fear and insecurity. A young girl's natural sexual need to explore or wear fun, flirty clothing can be suppressed by messages like "nice girls don't," which can inhibit her confidence on multiple levels later. Capricorn rules the passage of time, so with maturity this Venus often discovers a new playfulness, sexiness, and sensual confidence that she didn't have when she was younger. The years past midlife may be some of her more sexually alive ones, and, as partners discover, the natural tension that exists between her inhibitions and passions makes this sexually randy Venus sign a most exciting lover.

Introspective artistic activities are incredibly healing for Venus in Capricorn, who values time spent alone working on art forms, making the inner creative process tangible, as a path to joy, self-worth, and freedom. Any type of artistic work benefits Venus in Capricorn exponentially over time, as the persistent ongoing discipline of working with an art form allows her to know her true feelings thoroughly and overcome any self-doubt about her authority as a person and as a woman. As this Venus sign learns to trust her own responses and creative expressions as good and worthwhile, she heals her old fears of rejection and ridicule. Those who accept and love unconditionally, who do not judge or shame in any way, are also potent healers for this Venus sign.

Capricorn is the sign of work, and this Venus will work hard at developing professional and creative independence and autonomy. But Venus in Capricorn must take care to choose relationships and interests that express her true personal values, interests, and whims. Doing anything for the applause and appreciation of others is a trap for Capricorn; the only person's respect and love she needs to win is her own. Dependency on another person, for self-worth and lovability, is a sort of death for Venus in Capricorn. But liberated from a need for others, for their approval, she is free to enjoy, as Virginia Woolf did, the "enormous pleasure of being wanted."

A ROOM OF ONE'S OWN

Venus in Capricorn needs to be in a loving, interdependent relationship and yet not actually need the other person at all. If that sounds like a paradoxical task, it is—but not an impossible one! In a relationship, the thing she needs to learn most is to stand on her own two feet, to be self-reliant and trust her own authority.

As Virginia Woolf wrote, "A woman must have money and a room of her own if she is to write fiction." How does this need for a room of one's own play out in a relationship—a bond based on togetherness? An ideal relationship has three rooms: separate rooms for each person to lead a life independent of the other, and another room for the two to meet and come together as one. Rooms are bound spaces, so boundaries of space, time, and personhood need to be negotiated, understood, and honored in the relationship. Obviously, not everyone you meet will enjoy this style of self-reliant and committed yet interdependent partnership. But this Venus does.

So why is this evolutionary need so strong in Venus in Capricorn? She may have had a past relationship with a spouse who acted like an authoritative parent or, conversely, with someone who needed parenting from her or who encouraged dependency. Today, overly dependent, clingy, or needy individuals are real turn-offs, as is any person who resembles the archetype of an emotionally unavailable but judgmental father or mother figure. Because this Venus has had experiences with partners, priests, authorities, or family members who have judged or shamed her feelings and erotic desires, it's time for her to actually express her true emotions, needs, and desires to her partner. In the past, it was too easy to anticipate disappointment and judgment. Now, needs must be discussed and negotiated.

A Venus in Capricorn is learning self-sufficiency in relationships, and how good it feels to stand on her own two feet. This often translates as her earning her own income or having a career that makes her feel good about herself. Interdependence doesn't mean acting like a free agent (e.g., making important decisions without consulting her partner); what it does mean is that the partnership itself can provide the raw materials for that self-sufficiency to happen.

THINK WITH YOUR VENUS MANTRA, VENUS IN CAPRICORN

Love is the true foundation of my life's work. I form goals and reach my dreams with the support of my partner. I am blessed with the dedication and commitment to accomplish great things in life, and I know that together all things are possible.

YOU ARE MY ROCK

It's no surprise that Virginia Woolf wrote a book entitled *To The Lighthouse*. The lighthouse is a symbol of endurance: of light, guidance, protection, security, and shelter in stormy and uncertain weather. The image of the lighthouse speaks to both the Venus-in-Capricorn person and what she is attracted to in another. This earth Venus sign looks for partners with the qualities of stability, reliability, and maturity, because she possesses those strengths, too.

Venus in Capricorn's ideal mate is a person of substance. They may be formidable or have authority in the community, but they must possess great strength and steadiness in the face of life's storms. They must be in the relationship for the long haul and be dependable, reliable, and unwavering during times of uncertainty. It's tickling how often Venus-in-Capricorn people are heard referring to their partner as their "rock." It's a great compliment.

Just as a lighthouse provides clear light and direction for the ships in a storm to come ashore, Venus in Capricorn has a clear sense of what's real and what's not real in a relationship, other factors notwithstanding (a strong Neptune influence, for instance). Not prone to romantic daydreams and delusions about who her love interest or partner is, this Venus is realistic about her choice of partner and about her relationships. Sometimes Venus in Capricorn's attitude can be too sober and serious. When she stubbornly insists on having unyielding control of a situation or person, this Venus sign could benefit from bringing a bit of flexibility, fancifulness, daring, and spontaneity into the mix.

Like the lighthouse, this Venus sign can endure the testy, stormy weather of love and come out wiser for it. Not the type to lose her head to love, Venus in Capricorn will seriously weigh the impact of an impulsive romantic gesture or erratic desire against the long-term costs before she makes any sudden moves to enter or exit a relationship. Whether she begins or ends a relationship, this Venus will always fully understand the consequences set in motion as a result of her actions, even if that understanding is not apparent to others. A whimsical affair of the heart is not this person's forte; loyalty and long-term commitment are. If she decides to leave a committed relationship, she will generally do so with full knowledge of the financial and emotional consequences. In other words, she grasps the real-life implications of everything. Venus in Capricorn regards romantic partnerships the same way she regards fun: seriously.

Sunday Morning Love

Venus in Capricorn knows about the perils of responsibility that come with love. We marry young, before we know who we are, or accept the responsibility of becoming a mother, wife, and partner before we're ready. The specifics will vary, but the plotline is the same: Venus in Capricorn knows love is a willing obligation, one undertaken with eyes wide open, and that real love is not always romantic. There are bills to pay, careers to nurture, and family members to support.

Her ideal partner won't necessarily resemble Brad Pitt, and the partnership may at times lack the spontaneous qualities of carefree abandon we've all been socialized to think romance should have. Surely this Venus sign would enjoy a spontaneous love affair with a Brad Pitt lookalike, but it's not what she desires most, for while Venus in Capricorn loves romance as much as the rest of us, she needs a partner of substance. Her partner must be responsible and accomplished, demonstrate integrity, and be someone she admires and respects.

Virginia Woolf's marriage certainly wasn't always ponies and roses, but it did allow her to come into her own. Leonard Woolf—undoubtedly influenced by turn-of-the-century perceptions about women as the weaker sex as well as confusion surrounding mental illness at that time—often treated Virginia deferentially, like a child. Yet their respect and admiration for each another endured, forming the foundation of their powerful alliance. Through the lens of Capricorn, we can glimpse what works for a Venus-in-Capricorn marriage (creative partnership, boundaries, respect) and what is less important (quixotic adventures). The beauty of knowing your Venus sign is realizing that what will work for you may not work for someone else. For many Venus-in-Capricorn born, a committed relationship based on integrity and respect sets the foundation for real happiness to emerge.

Capricorn happiness is not the romance of Hollywood. A Venus-in-Capricorn relationship resembles less a grand, sweeping love affair than a partnering of two capable, caring individuals who are there for each other the morning after. Capricorn love isn't a happy-happy-joy-joy chemical rush and a dozen roses every other week, anyhow. It's having the privilege of sharing our morning coffee and paper with someone we truly love, honor, cherish, and respect, day in and day out. Venus in Capricorn specializes in sober Sunday morning love, and then does that steady-does-it love, seven days a week, twelve months a year.

THE BITTER AND SWEET

Venus in Capricorn is capable of having a relationship that endures growth challenges, changes in weather, and the kind of uncertainty any committed couple faces over a long stretch of time. This Venus appreciates a partner who can and will do the same for her—someone who has a strong grip on reality, deftly manages their money and career, and is an all-around model of self-sufficiency and maturity. In other words, her ideal partner is an adult in all ways, like she is. Maturity matters. Otherwise, this Venus sign can end up parenting a childlike partner instead of co-creating a dream life together.

Maturity isn't always tied to age, though sometimes it obviously is. Some souls seem to pop out of the womb as "wise souls" or "little adults" with a real-life ability to enjoy homework over video games. Venus-in-Capricorn born learn to appreciate the passage of time more deeply, because there are certain things, people, and ideas whose value we can only appreciate as we age, and as experience seasons us and distills into wisdom. Sometimes this means being with an older partner. More likely, this Venus has an appreciation for and finds greater pleasure in long-term companionship, the type that develops slowly over time.

In love and life, we taste the bitter to enjoy the sweet. Of all the Venus signs, Venus in Capricorn grows more body-confident with age and experience. She may have skipped over fun and folly in her youth, but as she ages she takes more risks and reaps the rewards. She didn't give up nor give in. She grew a backbone. No one did it for her, and in that she earns self-respect. As she matures over the years, her sensuality deepens like a fine wine. Any lingering insecurity holding her back gives way to gentle and sweet, full-bodied confidence and complexity. She melts, relaxes, and enjoys the time she has on Earth.

YOUR EROTIC STRENGTH

Capricious humor. When it comes to tempting things, people, and activities that turn others into malleable lumps of clay, you possess an enviable level of calm, cool, and collected self-control. Your dentist probably loves you for this. But (depending on whether the rest of your chart is more conservative or expansive) sometimes it's okay to live a little, to cut loose with a joke. Be fanciful. Get witty. Why not? Joie de vivre precipitates joy, and that relaxed and at-one-with-the-world feeling is the frequency at which love vibrates, my friend. Loosen your grip. Lose control. Laugh! Then cry! You know that moment in romantic comedies where the humble secretary takes off her glasses and becomes erotic, and more human? There's nothing sexier than a Venus in Capricorn letting her hair down.

IF YOU'RE IN LOVE WITH VENUS IN CAPRICORN...

Your Venus in Capricorn is a steadfast mate who wants to give you a lifetime of devotion, care, and mutual respect and looks for ardor, integrity, and sincerity in you. Professional support ranks high on her must-haves in a mate, so take her ambitions seriously and give her plenty of room to pursue her calling. If your love is true, write your wedding vows now—this Venus takes commitment seriously.

Venus in Capricorn is classically compatible with earth signs (Taurus, Virgo, Capricorn) and water signs (Cancer, Scorpio, Pisces) but, like Capricorn, Leo likes working toward goals. Whether in a working or romantic partnership, both share a stubborn streak and a natural affinity for teamwork.

Venus in Aquarius

~~

We're all a little weird. And life is weird.
And when we find someone whose weirdness is compatible
with ours, we join up with them and fall into mutually
satisfying weirdness—and call it love—true love.

~THEODOR GEISEL (DR. SEUSS), VENUS IN AQUARIUS

YOUR LOVE ELEMENT

All-knowing, clear, quixotic—air manages to be everywhere at once. Not wanting to be boxed in, air moves as swiftly as a breeze. An equal opportunist, air gets along just peachy with all the other elements in the zodiac: Air feeds fire's passions, causing fire's flames to leap higher. Air has great chemistry with water, as oxygen joins with hydrogen. The earth's biosphere relies on air to keep us earthlings alive; air blankets each and every corner and pocket of the earth, leaving no surface untouched or unknown. Indiscriminate air seems to be in everyone's business, existing everywhere all at once; yet air remains unbound, wild, and free. All-seeing and all-knowing, unassuming and clear, air is what it is.

Your Secret Desire

To peel back the shiny veneer of falsity in human relationships; to finally get real about what, how, and whom we choose to love—no matter what other people will think, do, or say. You, Venus in Aquarius, are ready to be fully seen for who you truly are. To accept this mission, a most radical act of self-love, you must be daring and truthful. This includes no longer asking for others' approval or permission to go your own way and do your own thing.

Your Love Charms

- Authenticity. You may not always know who you are, but you know who you are not. You win friends and influence people when you're being you.

- Your all-inclusive charm. It's in your nature to invite everyone into your inner circle. The more interesting, freaky, and fascinating they are, the better the fit for you.

- Your friendly love. You have a special place in your heart for the disenfranchised underdogs of the world. If there's a freedom-fighting cause, a story to tell, or a world to change, you generously offer your interest and friendship.

- Your unconventional tastes. In flavor, clothing, art, and style, your bumper sticker reads: "Why be normal?" Sometimes your irreverence shocks, but those people probably needed shaking up anyway.

- Your experimental, brainy style. You value knowledge about genes over designer jeans, but with your talent for making what's smart beautiful, your fashion and art experiments yield all kinds of weird science.

- You're a step ahead of the crowd. Whether a radical new trend or geeky new technology, you have your finger on the pulse of what's next. You especially enjoy questioning prevailing cultural, sexual, behavioral, and social norms.

- You're conversant and in the know. A great conversation about cutting-edge topics is mental foreplay for you. When your neural synapses light up brighter than a fireworks finale, you're relaxed and happy.

YOUR LOVE GODDESS

One of Venus's many roles is to inspire, as a muse. While a muse may be talked about, looked at, or even be the subject of controversy, her voice is heard through the filter of an artistic medium or another person's voice or gaze. The muse has no voice of her own. Gloria Steinem (b. 1934) would not become anyone's muse when, in an outrageous act of indignation on behalf of muses everywhere, she used her voice to speak and write about sexism.

For one of her most famous pieces, Gloria went undercover and worked as a Playboy Bunny at the Playboy Club in New York City, recording in great detail all the ways these women were being sexually exploited. Initially this article made her wildly unpopular; she was blacklisted by colleagues and unable to get a writing job for a long while. A Venus in Aquarius who is called to live by her own rules will be the unpopular outcast for a time. Every Venus sign wants to be liked and have the love and approval of family and peers, but the social and gender values of Venus in Aquarius swim against the prevailing current, placing her in the path of rejection and disapproval. What to do? If she's to be true to herself, Venus in Aquarius must endeavor not to be swayed by anyone's opinion of her.

Honoring one's unique personal truth and path is difficult in our society. At birth we are given a preset path to follow, and while that set of values varies by culture and family, none of us are immune. Maybe we are supposed to get married by age twenty-eight to a member of the opposite sex, have kids, join every committee we can, helicopter-parent our kids, have a great career, and look eternally young and skinny. We are awash in cultural programming long before we discover who we truly are. This can drive our life decisions, causing us to try to change who we are and deny our personal truths.

All of this pressure bears down on Venus in Aquarius's self-esteem and her relationship to her femininity and sexuality. She may conform to the rules for a while, but if you were born with Venus in Aquarius, there's something about "the rules" that doesn't fit your reality. Because this Venus embodies the archetypes of the rebel, alien, and exile, being true to herself also means risking rejection or being an outsider. Often this Venus sign will attempt to make others happy and appease them for as long as she can—until she wakes up and realizes just how much of her soul she is selling for the sake of a sense of belonging, security, and acceptance. She knows approval is not love. To claim the happiness and fulfillment she desires, Venus in Aquarius must annihilate her need for social approval, belonging, or fitting in. She can shave the edges off a square peg to fit in for a time, but eventually she learns that doing so is disingenuous and potentially disfiguring.

If this Venus is a rebel, it's for good reason. Venus civilizes, and while the Aquarian urge to liberate and reform can be confrontational or harsh, Venus smooths out rough edges, creating the urge for intelligent debate instead of arguments and using stylish acts of provocation to get her point across. By charming us with her outrageousness, this Venus makes the revolution of radical change attractive.

Outrage is sacred for Venus in Aquarius. Gloria Steinem provoked arguments and revolutionary dialogues about the nature of gender, sexuality, and race. Those with this Venus sign were born to challenge the status quo in terms of personal values, relationships, self-worth, and body image. This may include redrawing the lines of the sexual and body politic, redefining the social and gender roles within a community and the very definition of marriage, or breaking the relationship mold in a family lineage.

Venus in Aquarius's ardor for equality and truth (as she sees it) is unmatched. She offers agape, a universal form of friendly love, to everyone in the universe who needs it.

This is why she needn't worry about being unpopular forever. This Venus is born ahead of the times, intuitively knowing what's next, and since Aquarius's very personal choices and values are linked with the collective tide, which she initially challenges, eventually she sets a trend for others to follow. Still, you won't find her in the popular hangouts. By the time her fashion, fad, or movement goes mainstream, she's nowhere to be found. Venus in Aquarius has moved on.

OUTRAGEOUS BEAUTY

Venus, the planetary glyph, resembles a handheld mirror with a comb crossed over the handle (♀). When we look into Venus's mirror, who do we see? We see our inner relationship to our feminine sensuality, beauty, and self-esteem. Our Venus sign is the lens through which we measure or value ourselves.

Venus in Aquarius looks in the mirror and sees someone set apart, someone different from what society wants her to be.

Precisely because she needs to break free from oppressive values, gender roles, and limiting social constructs into which she was born, she sees a revolutionary in the mirror. As she sees herself, so she sees others, and she can take great pleasure in aligning herself with the outcasts or misfits of the bunch—any individuals or groups that are on the fringe of society, alienated, or different. With her revolutionary ideas about gender and social politics, she delights in breaking sexual and gender molds. She champions any human rights issue with charm, thoughtful clarity, and, above all, truthfulness.

Establishing rapport with others is a true Venusian power. Venus in Aquarius connects with others through her radical, often brilliant ideas and her deviant or avant-garde aesthetics. Venus-in-Aquarius-born Diane Arbus did this when she photographed social outcasts and misfits, forcing the viewer to confront the pain of being cast out and exiled. In so doing, Arbus performed an outrageous Venus act, awakening us to our own feelings of not fitting in, of being different. Outrageous acts of beauty like these have shaken the tree to the point of irrevocable change, as Gloria Steinem's *Playboy* article did. The human body can be just as provocatively radical as a political rally or a work of art. Sharon Stone, another Venus in Aquarius, was in full possession of her feminine sexuality in the film *Basic Instinct*. Her full-frontal crotch shot, a demonstration of sensual and sexual ownership, was truly unprecedented! For Venus in Aquarius, art, beauty, and her relationship to sexuality and self-worth are all tools for liberation—and ways for this Venus sign to change, if not revolutionize, the world.

Channeling her outrage into acts of outrageousness and radical self-love is healing for the Venus who has suffered oppression. Venus in Aquarius's perceptions about love, art, beauty, and sexuality are far from mainstream or ordinary. She's the one who wants to build a separate wing on the house for herself or her partner. Yet what's outrageous to one person is not necessarily the same to the next. Outrageous acts of beauty in Islamic countries aren't the same as in the United States; we are shaped by the cultural constructs of the time and place in which we live.

Whether it's taking off her burqa or leaving a stifling marriage, outrage is sacred to Venus in Aquarius. Standing up for her right to be happy, free, and loved in the way she wants to be loved is a radical act of self-love. When this Venus sign dares to turn the tables on social expectations, she will likely shock people. This certainly makes for interesting relationships. It also makes this Venus sign one of the most exciting and unusual people to hang with.

Venus in Aquarius might enjoy...
Your friends, radicals, geniuses, social networking, starting a revolution, the sciences, social experiments, self-actualization and individuation tools like life coaching, psychology, the enneagram, planning, looking into the future with astrology or tarot.

FEMININE REBELLION

In every revolution there's a danger of throwing out the baby with the bathwater, of eliminating the past for the new order. For instance, the sexual revolution gave freedom to women in groundbreaking ways, but there was also a subtle devaluation of traditional feminine arts like motherhood, cooking, and caring for and nurturing others. As women gained more freedom, baby making, childrearing, and feminine sensuality (with its emphasis on appearance and beauty) were often viewed as oppressive. Often, in order to correct an extreme, we need to reject the entire paradigm at first; but if this rejection occurs at the cost of our whole selves, that's not freedom—it's prison.

Venus in Aquarius is a revolutionary. If the oppression is an emotionally painful one, she can freeze up and become reactionary, which can cause a host of problems. Socially, she may react against the very people and things she wants to connect with, educate, and civilize. She may react against abuses and oppressions by abandoning her feminine nature or her body. In the extreme, if she's been sexually abused, she may disconnect from painful emotions associated with her body, preferring to relate through her mind instead and preventing any sexual or erotic connection from being made in intimacy. Venus in Aquarius can find it difficult to drop into her sensual body and emotions during sex, instead experiencing sex as a mental exercise. If she's been sexually violated and has unhealed sexual trauma, she may even leave her body altogether during sex.

Oppression is a reality for each and every woman. Many women have experienced walking down a street and receiving unwanted male attention and catcalls; many have feared for their lives simply because they are female. This is unfair and affects Venus's relationship to her feminine body, which can lead her to dissociate from her body or experience emotional disconnection in her relationships. Every Venus sign deserves to be rapturously, delightfully satisfied—socially, sensually, and intimately. Even if it takes a lifetime, she can work on healing the relationship to her feminine body. She can take a stand against oppressive people and ideologies and choose to remain connected to her femininity. She can choose partners who see her not just as a body, but as an intelligent thinker and an erotic, sensual woman. For a Venus who values freedom above all, these choices may be her most radical acts of all.

KARMIC LIBERATION

Every astrology textbook says Aquarius needs freedom. Why? Likely, it has been denied in the present or even past lives. In some major way, those exact things in our relationships that we most insist on today were probably denied, ignored, or even abused in the past. In the karmic past we may have signed on to play a role, to become someone we're not, to be a pretty face in the crowd, or we may have become overly defined by our gender role. We may have been regarded as a purely biological body, a baby-making machine, and not a complete person with emotional, psychological, and spiritual needs. Basically, in matters of relating and self-worth, we've deviated too far from our truth. This time around, Venus-in-Aquarius born are learning to trust the rudder of their own inner authenticity.

For Venus in Aquarius, all confrontations against her authentic self are opportunities for radical acts of outrage that bring her closer to happiness. Truthfulness is a perilous position for the goddess who strives for peace, love, and happiness, but Venus in Aquarius has no choice but to live by her own rules.

What freedom are you yearning for? What do you most want to be liberated from? Venus in Aquarius can sometimes be heard saying things like, "I want to be loved for my brains, not my body or my sexual orientation." This is a worthy request to make of her admirers and friends, but she should heed a gentle warning: over time, her reactionary insistence on being perceived in a certain way can bring out an intolerant streak in the sign known for its tolerance! This Venus should beware of rigid reactionary behavior; self-acceptance is the remedy for intolerance.

The liberation Venus in Aquarius craves isn't freedom from the expectations of others (every relationship has them), but the freedom to simply be herself. The deeper request of Venus always is: *Love me, for being me.* In Aquarius, Venus says, "I am unlike anyone you've ever known before. I will be real with you, and all I ask is for you to be authentic and real with me."

RADICAL ACCEPTANCE

I have a secret aphrodisiac especially for you, Venus in Aquarius. It's called acceptance. It's simple and underestimated and doesn't cost a thing. It's relaxing and easy to do, it puts others at ease, and it's sexy! After all, what's a bigger turn-on than being around someone who accepts you exactly as you are?

Acceptance is seductive for you. It greases the wheels of social discourse (and intercourse). It relaxes others. Your tolerant, open-minded nature helps you to connect to people you'd otherwise not get to interact with. They suddenly want to do your bidding, to please you. Bring an attitude of open acceptance to the table of business negotiations and watch closed doors open. Invoke a whiff of acceptance during an intimate moment and put a sexually shy or hesitant lover at ease.

Acceptance also heals relationship rifts. Acceptance always invites estranged friends in from the cold and back into the loving fold of companionship. While non-acceptance of a person's individual quirks and idiosyncrasies is a surefire way to lose friends, accepting someone for who they are is, simply put, a very good way to keep your friends. Radical acceptance is such a universal panacea that entire books have been written about it.

The true secret to activating the aphrodisiac of acceptance is, of course, accepting yourself first; that's the big work. If you accept others for who they are but don't accept yourself, you may find yourself in a promising relationship yet chronically stuck at the threshold of deep intimacy—precisely because you're too scared to be yourself. So accept your funky, eccentric, unusual, rebelliously intelligent self, Venus in Aquarius. That's how you attract people who value you for you.

THINK WITH YOUR VENUS MANTRA, VENUS IN AQUARIUS

I bring radical authenticity to the table of relationships, and the people who are still sitting there when I'm done are the ones I want in my life. I offer unconventionality and truthfulness to my partners. They love me for my irreverence and eccentricity.

ELECTRIC ROMANCE

Connection—how to connect with the right people—is all-important for Venus. Aquarius is an impersonal yet social air sign that typically likes to connect through groups, social networks, and technology. Internet dating, social networking, gaming, going out with friends of friends—all are very enjoyable ways for this Venus sign to connect with the people she loves.

The marvels of technology make it possible to connect with people in new ways and virtual scenarios, which this Venus sign loves, but technology can become problematic when we believe we're deeply connecting but we're not. To observe this, go to a restaurant and look at the number of people sitting at the same table talking not to one another but to someone else on their PDA. It's amazing how many people sit across from each other without really connecting. Likewise, online relationships can lose their luster in a face-to-face meetup when the person you thought you were getting to know really isn't that person. Of course this phenomenon doesn't necessarily entail electronics; two people can coexist side by side in a marriage without authentically connecting for decades. No Venus sign wants to experience that sad reality. An intimate partner with whom you can be your one-hundred-percent unadulterated, truthful self serves your deeper aim: authentic connection.

Day in and out, this Venus may be found flitting about with her social networks fulfilling goals and pursuing ideals and dreams among friends, but at the end of the day she wants someone solid and invested in the partnership, a life partner, to go home to. A partner who surprises and delights her, a stable someone she trusts implicitly but who will also keep her guessing, is erotically tantalizing for the Venus sign, who enjoys a bit of novelty and unpredictability. This Venus sign needs partners who stimulate her intellect and are natural truth-tellers. For Aquarius, there's nothing more attractive than intelligence. Aquarius is an intelligent air sign, so don't underestimate the power of shared mental chemistry. Mental rapport keeps this love fresh and exciting in the long term. There's nothing sexier than a mind-blowing conversation between two people who thought they really knew each other, only to discover something new. That's electrifying!

YOU ARE MY FRIEND

With your Venus in Aquarius, your friends and social network are all-important, so a bit of discernment is appropriate. Surrounding yourself with allies you admire is a surefire way to ensure your place among them, but the opposite is equally true. Spending time with people who need rescuing, aren't interested in heading in the same direction, or aren't reciprocal in their friendship will also ensure your place among them—but you may not be so happy about it.

This Venus sign has big dreams, and the right friends will help her fulfill those dreams. My advice? Gravitate toward the people you admire. Make a list of the people you look up to and want to emulate. Many of these people are probably your friends in your social network. What are their star qualities? Know that what you see uniquely in them is already yours. For proof positive of this, consider that even if you and I admired the same person, the traits we admired would be different.

Know that your most admired, accomplished friends aren't any more special than you are; they're simply holding up a mirror for your future self. The psychologist Carl Jung said there is an archetype called the "golden shadow" that exists in each of us. The golden shadow contains the bevy of desirable traits we covet in other people but believe we don't possess. If, according to wise man Jung, the qualities you most admire in others are those you already possess, there's only one thing to do: step into your future self by stepping out with your friends.

RADICAL SELF-LOVE

From feminist Gloria Steinem to the phenomenal singer Susan Boyle, who took to the world stage and proved talent trumps popstar fluff, when we are true to who we are, we have an effect on others that liberates them to be themselves, too. Yet how can we achieve true liberation without a confrontation with something that goes radically against our true nature?

Venus in Aquarius can define herself against an ideology—or even a loved one. Sometimes we accuse others of stifling us when we are the ones stifling ourselves. *J'accuse!* Don't demand that others grant you the freedom that is already yours; they are not your jailers. Consider that the thing that vexes you so is a thing of beauty, for it will lead you back to your true nature.

Aquarius is an experimental sign, and your willingness to experiment and see where it leads makes you magnetic. Venus merely wants you to enjoy the whole crazy thing, to boldly go forth into new territory, to take your pleasure, with pleasure. Don't be afraid to experiment with new and different social roles and self-images. Want to body-paint naked? Want to wear a tutu while walking the dog in Central Park? Okay, then. Truly, no one's opinion matters but yours, and the more you get the hang of giving yourself permission to be you, the happier and more content you will feel. Don't wait for your partner, or the world, to change so you can finally be that person you already are: exciting, freedom-loving, wild, and rebellious.

Radical Self-Love Credo

We, Venus-in-Aquarius born, need freedom to experiment with our erotic desires and peculiar pleasures. In doing so, we discover who we truly are.

We, who are so good at cataloging and observing all the funny, awkward, shy, and weird moments of our social and sexual interactions, can relax into our soft, sensual bodies, breathe into our hearts, and open to receive pleasure.

We, who are attracted to people who are outrageous by society's standards, know that the right people playfully liberate us so we can more fully be ourselves.

We, who are vulnerable to not being seen for who we truly are, choose not to allow insecurity or fear to guide our choices.

We practice radical self-acceptance. The right friends and communities encourage self-acceptance, but acceptance always begins at home.

YOUR EROTIC STRENGTH

Authenticity. To be an individual, we must "know thyself." What is a self, anyhow? In some schools, knowing our "self" means having a sense of our divinity and unique destiny in life. The original alchemists believed that having a substantial and reliable sense of self has a catalytic effect on others and on the world, which makes sense. When we have a reliable sense of self, we aren't afraid that loving another will cause us to lose ourselves. Acts originating from our unique self-essence extend far beyond what we personally sense and see and have an awakening effect on others. Does this thought make you happy? I bet it does. You can make the world a better place by being you.

IF YOU'RE IN LOVE WITH VENUS IN AQUARIUS...

Your Venus in Aquarius may need carte blanche to pursue her visions, dreams, and goals, but the planet of stability, Saturn, co-rules this sign (along with Uranus), so offer her both autonomy and your commitment. This intellectually provocative and exciting Venus sign is full of surprises; your life together is guaranteed never to be dull. Just don't get in between her and her wide circle of besties.

Venus in Aquarius is classically compatible with air signs (Gemini, Libra, Aquarius) and fire signs (Aries, Leo, Sagittarius), but pragmatic and clear-thinking Capricorn could be a fine match, too. Though each will find the other unyielding at times, they can meet in the middle to support each other's visions.

Venus in Pisces

♓

Love recognizes no barriers. It jumps hurdles, leaps fences,
penetrates walls to arrive at its destination full of hope.

~MAYA ANGELOU, VENUS IN PISCES

YOUR LOVE ELEMENT

Changeable, accepting, merging water moves fluidly from one form to another, easily transitioning from cloud to raindrop to sea. Forever changing form but not essence, water passes through barriers that are impossible to cross in any other way. Water knows no boundaries. Indiscriminately merging with anything and everyone, water unifies. It's in its nature to connect and merge. Water is generous, sometimes a little too generous, overflowing with bounty and causing a flood. Yet a stable earthen container or seawall finds water committed to taking shape as a reflecting pool, cove, or lake. Just as the sea refuses passage to no one, water accepts all who come its way. Water accepts all walks of life, and we gratefully surrender and open to this healing element.

YOUR SECRET DESIRE

To restore soulfulness and enchantment to the heart of a relationship. To mystify, beautify, and inspire where other lovers have fallen short, erotically and spiritually. To share your spiritual connection to all of life, with everyone you meet. Ambitious? Yes, but you're spiritually wired for this. And when you glimpse eternity while gazing into your beloved's eyes, that's your desire, fulfilled.

YOUR LOVE CHARMS

- Your otherworldly presence. You believe that having your third eye open and keeping your chakras clear is beautifying, good for your relationships, and good for the planet.

- Your graceful fluidity. The way you glide from situation to situation and person to person with poise and adaptability wins you friends and fans.

- You're a chameleon. You morph into any character that comes in handy in a variety of circumstances. In your mind's eye, you see life as a movie, a divine comedy, and you continually adapt your part in it.

- Your ability to love and let go. Whether you lose a limb or your heart, you have the ability to grow a new one, just like a starfish. "Better to have loved and lost than never to have loved at all" is programmed into your DNA.

- Your spiritual intimacy with life. Your intimate relationships improve in proportion to the level of intimacy you have with your spiritual life.

- Your generosity. Whether helping a sick friend or being there for your partner, you are supportive, ably offering time, affection, and attention. Your natural empathy and spiritual generosity make others feel seen.

- You're enchanting. With the imagination of a poet, the dreamy vision of an Impressionist painter, the romanticism of a love novelist, and the fantasy life of J. R. R. Tolkien, you can make it happen if you can dream it up.

FROM MUSE TO GODDESS

One day, we will all return to our Source. Whether we call that place Nirvana, Heaven, or Soul School, and whether we're Christian, Hindu, or Pagan, we probably all share similar ideas about what we will find there: connection, reunion, and love. Peeling back layers of dogmatic grime and human misunderstanding, we see that love is at the core of every faith and every heart.

Love and faith: they're what it takes to survive being human. Being human is no picnic; it's downright difficult. We all have a bevy of spiritual tasks to accomplish—tasks mired in human conditions that challenge us at our very core to go beyond our perception of them. These journeys are necessary for our soul growth. We all have the capacity to develop a more spiritual understanding of life; it isn't easy, but for some people it's essential to their evolution. For Venus in Pisces, developing this spiritual perception makes all the difference between being consumed by pain and discovering enlightened happiness.

Maya Angelou (1928–2014) was born into Earth School with a full list of spiritual growth tasks disguised as devastating challenges. Denied any advantage of privilege, Maya was born an African-American woman into an impoverished, uneducated, and abusive environment. Maya was shuffled between relatives during her entire childhood, and was abused and raped at age eight by her mother's boyfriend. After Maya found the courage to tell her brother about the abuse, it is believed that Maya's uncle beat her mother's boyfriend to death. Believing her voice caused a man to die, Maya refused to speak for almost five years. She eventually spoke again under the nurturing tutelage of a teacher who encouraged her to explore literature.

How did Maya survive? This Venus must seek the spiritual in the everyday, making the spiritual more real than what is in front of her. She must actively look for proof of miracles, goddesses, fairies, angels, light beings, and ascended avatars with her own mind, her consciousness. She must look for them in everyday mundane life, from a teaching moment in a traffic jam to the heart-shaped foam on her latte. She must look in difficult circumstances that rob many people of the very things she's blessed with: faith and belief. Venus in Pisces must develop spiritual values to guide her earthly experiences, values like "I am imperfectly perfect" and "all paths lead to love." No mere affirmations, these must become real values, a way of connecting to life, because when Venus in Pisces develops her spiritual third eye, she understands a deep secret: that life is an illusion, and true freedom is a leap of consciousness away.

Maya Angelou shares her name with another maya: *maya* is the Sanskrit word for "illusion." Great spiritual teachers know that life is an illusion—a really convincing dream. Maya's muse works in this way: it convinces us to believe that appearances and circumstances are our true reality. Maya is as convincing as the lies of a lover whom we want to believe even as we hear a whisper saying otherwise. When maya, or illusion, takes root in our consciousness, it uses our very eyes and minds to misguide us, yet because we are born awake, we have enough awareness to question ourselves even as we perpetuate false patterns of reality. Venus in Pisces finds it so easy to slip into this half-awake, half-dreaming state of muddled confusion, as bewilderment and uncertainty keep her stuck in inertia and inner passivity. Venus in Pisces also has the spiritual awareness to transcend maya by directing her life through a personal set of spiritual values.

Perhaps Maya Angelou would have had a greater chance of becoming a monster over a masterful writer had she believed the illusions. Her against-all-odds life is an inspiration, reminding us that no circumstance ever defines who we are. Nothing destroys our divinity. The astrological glyph for Pisces is the sign of the Fishes, who eternally swim in circles (♓). If we get caught in the Fishes' snare of illusion, we can swim in circles and spin our wheels. We may even spend an entire lifetime in confusion—forgetting, rather than remembering, who we are. But Pisces is also the sign of consciousness, and all it takes to detach ourselves from our own suffering is a shift in consciousness. When Venus in Pisces embarks on a path of meaningful spiritual discovery, she still experiences life as a fluid, ever-changing experience, but she is no longer chaotically tossed about on its sea. Her focused imagination becomes magnetic and her visions take flight. The love, the reality, the life she most desires no longer exists hidden away in her imagination. It has become more real than the tree standing outside her door.

EARTH ANGEL

Imagine that you had a sacred conversation with all of your soulmates and karmic mates before you were born. You all agreed to be in one another's lives on Earth, to teach each other soul lessons. It's not a far-flung theory. Studies say the majority of people in the world today believe in reincarnation, even despite religious differences. It's intriguing that such a large number of people believe in something that cannot be proven. Those with Venus in Pisces find it easy to entertain the possibility of psychic phenomena, the supernatural, and afterlives, because they have an inkling that this life is not the only movie in town.

In order for Venus in Pisces to let in more of what she wants to create in her life, she needs to have her world and mind expanded. The more time she spends exploring her inner perceptions, the more she fosters a sense of spiritual congruency in her life and in her relationships. She also experiences more of the expansive power of her own consciousness to make her happy. Switching focus from the outer to the inner experience can be as simple as making the space and time for just being. Sitting on a porch swing, lying in bed, or staring into another's eyes—these simple activities allow one's consciousness to observe and explore its own subtleties. Whether meditating or staring at the wall together with her partner, this Venus is looking for a quality of soulful connection with a person, idea, or thing she loves, one not typically fostered by our fast-paced modern lifestyle.

Unless you live in a monastery, it's not easy to find time for soulful connection. On planet Earth, we're busy. We also tend to believe only in what we can see, taste, and touch. We pay far too much attention to what's in front of our eyes rather than the infinite possibility contained between them—in our mind's eye! To function optimally, any planet in the sign of Pisces must have its imagination tickled, and its extra senses (beyond all five) opened and stimulated. How will this happen if we're too busy making plans for the weekend, too busy with the madness of human activity? The imagination and the world of fantasy, spirituality, and the supernatural are keys to Venus in Pisces' happiness and joy. In this lifetime, Venus in Pisces needs to believe in something beyond the "real" world, with its attendant list of responsibilities and identities. Karmic chances are she hasn't spent enough time in a delicious, rapturous, enchanting relationship with the Great Mystery. Now is her chance to awefully gaze with wonder at life and love.

Venus in Pisces might enjoy...

Concerts, make-believe, fantasy, movies, developing your psychic ability, making art, poetry, privacy, beds and bedrooms, essential oils, candles, daydreaming, color therapy, spa days, spiritual retreats, meditation, spiritual writings and teachings.

Fantasy Lover

The key to Venus in Pisces' happiness rests in the space between her ears: in her mind's eye. Here, in her conscious imagination, she lives a rich, full, vibrant life. Daydreaming and imagination are fodder for her sensuality. To feel sensually alive, Venus in Pisces needs a fantasy life like a fish needs water.

Erotic writer Anaïs Nin, a Venus in Pisces, had such an elaborate fantasy life that she was married to two men at the same time! Nin referred to her marriages as the bicoastal trapeze. Her life became so complicated that she had to create something she called the "lie box." She said, "I tell so many lies I have to write them down and keep them in the lie box so I can keep them straight."

Venus in Pisces may have a fantasy life or, like Anaïs, actually lead one. The lines blur between the images and impressions she absorbs from influences and people around her, and between who she believes herself to be and who she becomes. She can live her relationship life as though in a movie, literally becoming the characters of her imagination by creating the image of a relationship, or herself, in her mind's eye. She can also remain faithful to that vision of herself and the relationship even when it differs from the other person's experience. With this same ability, she can create ecstatic worlds of beauty, transporting us to fantastical places we love to dream about, hear about, read about, or visit. Thus she shares her Venus sign with many great artists, people who move fluidly between fiction and reality.

RETREAT AND RESTORE

If you've ever watched a movie and walked away feeling like you actually lived the experience, you understand how it feels to be a Pisces. Now imagine going to a family reunion afterward, your consciousness never having had the time to digest the movie you'd just seen, and here comes Uncle Jack along with your family's dysfunctional dynamics. You'd probably want to hide! Pisces planets live in a constant state of full-on absorption, which can be positively pleasurable or downright exhausting. It's no wonder this sign is notorious for escapism.

Venus in Pisces merges so easily with others that just as a droplet of water merges with the sea, so can she unconsciously become absorbed into another. This phenomenon can occur with an intimate lover whose characteristics, hobbies, and passions she adopts as her own, which can be both blissful and scary. One day they may be two peas in a pod, alike in every way, and the next day, when she and her lover part, Venus in Pisces may feel bereft of identity and purpose. Fortuneteller astrologers will say this Venus sign is particularly vulnerable to codependency, addiction, fantasy lovers, and losing herself to, and being absorbed by, others. This quality of boundary-less-ness, this urge to merge, is the cause.

Venus in Pisces' easy ability to go with the flow instead of controlling it can be a great strength with people and in circumstances requiring great flexibility; but when she gets too swept up in the drama of external forces, she becomes unmoored, and that strength turns into a weakness. When Venus feels tossed about like a piece of driftwood at sea, she benefits from cultivating her spiritual and inner life. Alone time allows Venus in Pisces to reevaluate her true values: *What is most important to me? Does this guide my choices, or are other people's values guiding me?* Then, from that centered and still place inside, she can choose anew.

Retreat restores Venus in Pisces. It removes those external forces—the people, information, and energy—that get in the way of her conscious awareness. Most of all, pleasurable retreat time allows her mind to drift on her own delta waves, not on someone else's. In silent reverie, she can witness her own mind and marshal the spiritual guidance she needs to make new choices and entertain new perceptions and possibilities. Through alone time, Venus in Pisces reevaluates her true values (*What is most important to me? Does this guide my choices, or are other people's values guiding me?*) and then chooses from that place.

BOUNDLESS LOVE

Venus-in-Pisces born are generous with their affections. When they love, they love liberally—they will give you the shirt off their back and support you emotionally, materially, and spiritually, in any way they can. If a friend needs to be driven to a doctor's appointment or a mutual acquaintance's pet needs to be looked after while they go on vacation, Venus in Pisces happily volunteers her services. Are blood donations needed at the Red Cross today? Is disaster relief needed in the Bahamas? She's all over it. Call her a sucker for a sob story, but she gets deep satisfaction from lending a helping hand.

Yet the same characteristics that make this Venus sign so beautiful can be her downfall when offered without discernment. She's learning to balance soulful, spiritually generous love with grounded realism. At best, maybe she's just a little spacy or loose with her time, money, and affections, sometimes causing trouble at her bank or with friends, work, and partners. At worst, this Venus finds herself romantically attracted to people who need her help, creative people who have emotional problems or have a poor relationship with reality. She may fall in love for the right reasons, believing she's found her soulmate, and, when reality rears its ugly head, end up maintaining the relationship out of guilt, obligation, or any number of misguided spiritual reasons, like believing "we share karma together." When that happens, a love that was so magical and enchanting at the beginning turns into martyrdom for this Venus.

Venus in Pisces can easily look past another's carefully constructed identity, behaviors, mannerisms, and style and truly see the beauty in the person's soul. It is lovely to see beauty in the soul of another, but if Venus sees only their beauty and then commits to someone who is financially irresponsible, has emotional health or addiction issues, etc., she will be in for a big reality check. By selectively focusing on one aspect of a person, she misses the whole picture.

The trick for Venus in Pisces is to keep her vision clear and her third eye open. As a balance to her hopeless romantic streak and spiritual generosity, a sense of realism and discernment must be developed. Instead of focusing solely on someone's beauty, she needs to try to see the whole person—flaws, warts, questionable habits, bank statements, and all—so she isn't disillusioned or even devastated by them later. This doesn't mean she should reject partners outright; we're all humanly flawed and imperfect. It does mean she needs to go into a relationship with her eyes wide open. If she's having trouble doing that, a grounded, earthy friend—someone with Virgo or Capricorn planets especially—could be the friend she needs most. Venus-in-Pisces born can have some of the most spiritually, soulfully connected, enchanted partnerships around, but to do this they must endeavor to look beyond the illusion of appearances—even when they think they've got it covered.

Think with Your Venus Mantra, Venus in Pisces

My outlandish, magnificent, and soulful diversions are enchantments that inspire others to no end. Whatever I ask for from love, I receive, and each day I become wiser in my desire. As I identify who and what I don't want in my life, I picture who and what I do want in my mind. The divine obliges my every wish.

Enchanted Play

Imagine you were talking to your angels in the time between lives, before you came down to Earth. Imagine these angels gave you a primer on the pitfalls and pains of planet Earth. The list was long. Then, in an aromatic whiff of roses, spicy bergamot, and fresh vanilla, Venus walked into the room, calmly announcing all would be well. The gods and goddesses, instantly cheered and relaxed by her presence, agreed (while chuckling over their inside joke that Venus is Mother Nature's valium). Then Venus took your arm and said the following:

"Want to know my secret? Keep your attention light and joyful, your mind open, and your imagination nourished by beauty, art, and nature. I have a special bit of advice for you, Venus in Pisces, and you will want to use it when you're feeling world-weary, stressed, or uninspired. Play soulful music to remember your soul. Dance to remember your own harmony. Meditate on what moves you. Move toward whatever and whoever brings you delicious and ecstatic soul rapture. But when you feel consumed or overwhelmed, take time alone to fill the well of your own bliss. The magic is within you. Cultivate an appreciation for that human condition called longing, without needing to fill it. Longing feeds the soul. Kiss the birds and the bees and the sky. Laugh. Remember that this world is temporary, so find your true Om."

Excited to have the attention of the goddess of love, you press your luck, asking, "But what about my soulmates? How will I recognize them?" She indulges you:

"You have a gift. When you're quiet enough, sometimes you can hear the trees speak and the flowers hum. You can hear a choir of angels in the silence of an old church. During a certain time of day, you see magic and you see it everywhere. This sense of magic, this enchantment with life, increases the longer you live. This gift connects you to all of life. But you must remember that not everyone has the ears to hear what you hear or the eyes to see what you see. Be friends with all of life, but only make your home with those people who have the ears to hear what you hear and the eyes to see what you see. Choose a partner who shares your love for the mystical, magical, fantastical, and supernatural, because these things bring you great pleasure—and shared pleasure is the basis of all loving connection. Otherwise, you may spend the rest of your life trying to reach someone who is just not capable of being reached."

MYSTIC PIZZAZZ

In traditional astrology, Venus is exalted in Pisces, which means Venus wears her finest clothes in this sign. Venus in Pisces is generous, empathic, mystical, soulful, an appreciator of art, and a connoisseur of exquisite beauty. While blessed with all these beautiful gifts, a person with this Venus can have a difficult time making her finer qualities work for her. Venus in Pisces is often humble, sensitive, and sometimes unable to understand her relationships, but when she consciously embodies her natural mysticism, she's simply dazzling.

Venus in Pisces is wired for a spiritually rich soulmate relationship. A relationship revolving exclusively around mundane nine-to-five routines, with little outlet for soulful spirituality and fantastic revelry, leaves this Venus unhappy and energetically dissipated. When this happens, she can become a martyr, serving time in the relationship. She may also invent a new one; no Venus sign is better at creating a fantasy relationship than Venus in Pisces. When she gets caught up in a fantasy movie of her own making instead of enchanting the real world with her wonder and spiritual curiosity, her love life turns into a web of self-deception and unhappiness. It seems that no one and nothing can save her, save a change in her own consciousness.

With your Venus in Pisces, your great potential lies in cultivating a number of meaningful relationships in which you can connect on a soul and spiritual level—but without the damaging albatross of addiction, delusion, self-deception, or martyrdom. The quickest way to do this, of course, is to attract a person heading in the same direction, on the same spiritual path, and at the same level of consciousness as you are. But if you're in a difficult relationship rut, try entertaining a more mystical perception about it. In the spirit world, just as in the human world, like attracts like. Instead of seeing your relationship (or your partner) as a problem, try seeing it as a reflection of something you need to look at inside yourself. Is the relationship serving a need for you? Is your partner giving you an opportunity to grow in a new direction—to reach out and explore a new path, to write a book, to use your gifts in new ways? Take a more empowering perspective on this relationship.

If you're looking to spice up your love life, develop your psychic abilities. Attend a spiritual class. Squeeze crystals. Do Goddess yoga. You can imagine your lover into reality. There's no sign more able to conjure up a new love, or anything at all really, so don't forget that you can always attract new people and experiences with the power of your imagination. Anything is possible for you. Make a bid for more enlightened relationships by keeping your chakras open, your karma clear, and your love light bright and shiny. That's how you find your mystic pizzazz!

YOUR EROTIC STRENGTH

Wonder. Ever wonder if Heaven exists and, if it does, what it looks like? If there's a place where the sun shines year round? Ever wonder what the color of your aura is? The open-ended question *Ever wonder...?* has inspired new thoughts, adventures, and many maiden voyages. Nothing in the world can be created without wonder! What does wonder look like to you? If wonder were a taste, would it be your mother's recipe for marshmallow divinity? How will you fill your heart with wonder? Start counting the ways, today. As a pursuit, there's nothing more fulfilling than exploring the wonders of the world. An attitude of wonder makes you attractive. In fact, the more you explore your world and all its wonders, the more wonderful you feel, and the more wonderful others find you. Wonder is always beautiful. Wonder is just wonder-full.

If You're in Love with Venus in Pisces...

Your Venus in Pisces promises you that life with her will be enchanting, a mystical trip to the outermost regions of your erotic and intellectual imaginations where you can be sylphs, mermaids, or Bonnie and Clyde together. Empathic and generous, this Venus sign doesn't hesitate to give you everything. She also can't resist a stray in need, so make sure your love nest has a guestroom.

Venus in Pisces is classically compatible with water signs (Cancer, Scorpio, Pisces) and earth signs (Taurus, Virgo, Capricorn), though she and Sagittarius both share a lust for adventure and a desire to turn their wildest dreams into reality. Their magical mating could take love to the next level.

Conclusion

*Ginger Rogers did everything Fred Astaire did,
except backwards and in high heels.*

~COMMONLY ATTRIBUTED TO BOB THAVES

I wrote this book for those of us who need a boost of self-love, especially for women (though I hope men find the information in this book equally useful). Women have historically been socialized to focus on others' happiness—a skill that ensures the survival of the species but can also hold us back. This shows up in our partnerships in small ways, but the impact it has on our quality of life is big. We don't ask for what we desire and then resent others for getting what they want. We make having our desires met dependent on another's approval. Instead of respecting ourselves and acting on our needs, wants, joys, and desires, we complain about feeling disrespected by our partners. We don't slow down and relax and enjoy ourselves. Instead of honoring our desires and valuing ourselves enough to take what we want seriously, we make demands on our partners. And we wonder why we're unhappy.

Venus can be gracious, acquiescing, and kind when the situation calls for it, but not as a way of life. Making others happy, pleasing other people, is definitely a valuable feminine skill set, but Ginger didn't dance for Fred's sake. Ginger danced for her own pleasure. A healthy Venus never forgets to make her own desires central.

We've come a long way since the sexual revolution, but we may need to relearn some of the lessons our mothers and grandmothers brought to light. Living authentically is the call of modern times, yet women face unique challenges to "unleashing our power" and "living our potential," as so many self-help experts tell us we should be doing. Many of us still feel we are falling short, that we aren't doing something magnificent with our newfound freedoms. Maybe we are feeling "less than" because we still aren't all that free. These oppressions creep up in our intimate partnerships. Maybe you've noticed how your male counterparts assume they will have their needs met while women often agonize over claiming a small crumb for themselves. Or how sometimes when a woman enters a logic-driven conversation and communicates her point of view by expressing her feelings, experience, and intuition, her opinion is dismissed and not taken seriously. Oppression is real; it is an underpinning of all of our relationships, whether we see it or not.

Feminine strength comes from the inside, but how free we feel to express ourselves can limit us, keeping it inside. To experience strength, we need to let it out. We don't have to wait for our marriage to fall apart, for the epiphany "I forgot to claim a crumb for/value myself!" We don't have to wait to be tested in order to discover that we have inner strength. Iconic dress designer and seductress Diane Von Fürstenberg (a Venus in Scorpio), when asked how things have changed for women, said, "You know the situation with women is very much on a pendulum. All I can tell you is that I've never met a woman who is not strong, but sometimes they don't let it out. Then there's a tragedy, and then all of a sudden that strength comes. My message is let the strength come out before the tragedy."

As simple as it sounds, the act of courageously pursuing what we enjoy can tap our inner strength and help us take a leap of confidence. For instance, consider flirting—one of the greatest feminine powers we have. Remember this from grade school? When you flirted, you didn't demand that your love interest notice you, but instead you became playfully curious, you let go of expectations and opened to whatever happened next—*you flirted*. It's time to flirt with your own Venus. Flirt with the people you love, the people you want to love, and the person you'd like to become. Flirt with the desires, pleasures, charms, and eroticism of your Venus sign. To be deliciously happy, we must flirt, love, and laugh with abandon—be promiscuous with all of life.

Women face real oppressions, but with consciousness we can love and laugh with the abandon of Aphrodite. We may decide to dance backwards in high heels, but we don't have to bend over backwards to please—and we don't have to let our desire for approval constantly throw us off center. We can take a cue from mighty Aphrodite, whose throaty laughter and flirty jokes reach back from history all the way to us. Aphrodite, like Ginger Rogers, made it look easy. Maybe it is.

For Further Understanding

For the most comprehensive understanding of your Venus, book an astrology session with an astrologer—like me. You can learn more about my customized personal and relationship readings at Moonkissd.com.

The following were consulted while writing *Venus Signs*. I highly recommend them:

Bolen, Jean Shinoda. *Goddesses in Everywoman: Powerful Archetypes in Women's Lives.* New York: HarperCollins, 2004.

Dreyer, Ronnie Gale. *Venus.* London: Aquarian Press, 1994.

Forrest, Steven and Jodie. *Skymates: Love, Sex, and Evolutionary Astrology.* Chapel Hill, NC: Seven Paws Press, 2002.

Gerhardt, Dana. Venus article series at Astrodienst. www.astro.com/astrology/in_venus_e.htm.

Green, Jeffrey Wolf. *Pluto: The Soul's Evolution Through Relationships, Volume 2.* St. Paul, MN: Llewellyn, 1997.

Shepherd, Jessica. *A Love Alchemist's Notebook: Magical Secrets for Drawing Your True Love into Your Life.* Woodbury, MN: Llewellyn, 2010.

Appendix 1: Good Witch, Bad Witch

Here is a summary of light and shadow traits of each Venus sign.

VENUS IN ARIES, GOOD WITCH

- Takes emotional risks: shares the good, the bad, and the ugly emotions
- Honors her need for change and adventure
- Consciously chooses worthy adversaries—challenging, fun partners who empower confidence, not competition
- Learns to ask what she can give to the relationship
- Learns to fight fair

VENUS IN ARIES, BAD WITCH

- Love daredevil (too impulsive) or shrinking violet (too shy)?
- Restless in love; loses interest easily
- Too many false starts in relationships

- Provokes arguments that chip away at happiness
- Focuses on what the relationship/partner isn't giving her

VENUS IN TAURUS, GOOD WITCH

- Uses her body knowledge to make choices: "How does this feel in my body?"
- Enjoys pleasure, money, food, and sex, but knows they are not the source of her security
- Gravitates toward nature environments and animals for calm and peace
- Takes risks in sharing her resourceful talents
- In dating and sex, takes it slow and easy

VENUS IN TAURUS, BAD WITCH

- Insecurity with body
- Feeds need for comfort and grounding with food
- Prefers stability over growth in partnerships
- Can be too insecure to put her talents out there
- Knotty self-worth issues around money and deservedness

VENUS IN GEMINI, GOOD WITCH

- Gives expressive, experimental, provocative, and creative side free rein
- Plays the field, explores, dates around
- Consciously chooses to gather experience before committing to one person
- Chooses interesting, curious, open-minded, mentally stimulating partners

Venus in Gemini, Bad Witch

- Boredom, restlessness, ambivalence in love
- Chronically torn between two partners
- Chooses closed-minded, uninteresting partners
- Goes in circles with her talents; no clear direction
- Circles the appetizer table but never arrives at the main course: intimacy

Venus in Cancer, Good Witch

- Doesn't placate or seek approval from parents or partners
- Chooses tender, romantic, sensitive, nurturing, emotionally available mates
- Caretaking is mutual, a two-way street
- Knows that sharing emotions creates intimacy
- Uses shell to retreat and heal, not hide

Venus in Cancer, Bad Witch

- Regards super-sensitivity as a liability
- Hides out in shell, afraid to open up emotionally
- Dates mama's boys and the walking wounded
- Takes care of others and neglects herself
- Doesn't leave home; unhealthy family-of-origin dynamics dominate partnership

Venus in Leo, Good Witch

- Understands that the need for praise, affection, and applause is human and worthy

- Spontaneously and generously shares herself
- Chooses romantic partners who consistently express adoration, praise, and affection
- Celebrates love every day; waking up next to her is like Christmas morning every day

Venus in Leo, Bad Witch

- Feels shame around self-expression
- Hungers to be recognized and loved but doesn't feel special enough
- Demands affection, and creates drama if she's not getting it
- Hides brilliance, beauty, charisma, and joy behind façade of invisibility (we see you!)

Venus in Virgo, Good Witch

- Sees perfection as an aspiration, not a reality
- Doesn't let relationship grievances pile up
- Love is expressed through mutual responsibility to the partnership and each other's happiness
- Chooses partners who model acceptance, surrender, and forgiveness, and learns to do this for herself

Venus in Virgo, Bad Witch

- Feels either inadequate to others or superior to them
- Chooses partners who shame, nitpick, criticize
- Critical; complains
- Busybody; has a hard time relaxing
- Worries and frets over perceived relationship obstacles

VENUS IN LIBRA, GOOD WITCH

- Sees conflict as a natural result of what happens when two universes collide
- Easily tolerates the paradox that loving someone doesn't mean the two have to agree
- Uses empathy and negotiation to resolve conflicts
- Chooses to be with an equal who values a mutual, civilized, democratic style of partnering

VENUS IN LIBRA, BAD WITCH

- Won't rock the boat with conflict—too unpleasant
- Values the icing on the cake, even if the substance of the relationship lacks fulfillment
- Tries to make everyone happy all the time, to the detriment of her own happiness
- Puts partner on a pedestal; shocked when the person turns out to be human

VENUS IN SCORPIO, GOOD WITCH

- Empathically and compassionately opens up about charged taboo topics, and supports others revealing their secrets, too
- Psychologically sophisticated; knows her own shadow
- Has an empowered relationship to sexuality
- Willing to shed old skin and stagnant, toxic relationships when necessary for growth
- Is unwaveringly loyal to those she loves

VENUS IN SCORPIO, BAD WITCH

- Engages in power struggles instead of being honest
- Venus envy; may be unaware of her own power, eroticism, and magnetism
- Sabotages relationships by giving her fears authority
- Is either obsessed with her partner or unforgiving
- Controls, manipulates, or dominates others

VENUS IN SAGITTARIUS, GOOD WITCH

- Has an appetite for life and experience; surrounds herself with diverse, interesting people
- Views a committed relationship as a vehicle for growth, wisdom, new perspectives, and discovering a new kind of freedom
- Is up for and willing to try anything
- Chooses adventurous mates who like to have a good time and are motivated by philosophical and spiritual growth

VENUS IN SAGITTARIUS, BAD WITCH

- Thinks freedom and commitment are mutually exclusive
- A rolling stone gathers no moss—or intimacy
- Hung up on one truth, path, or ideology
- Chooses sexually restrained, closed-minded partners

VENUS IN CAPRICORN, GOOD WITCH

- Values self-sufficiency in partnerships; loves someone without needing the person
- Takes vows with mature, committed partners

- Has a room of her own, for solitary creative pursuits; develops her own authority
- Uses humor and play to lighten things up
- Reclaims sexuality and self-worth from shaming or judgment

Venus in Capricorn, Bad Witch

- Early social, religious, and/or family conditioning instills an attitude of social or sexual correctness
- Spontaneity can be difficult, controlled; consults inner rule book for appropriate response
- Relationship only revolves around work and responsibilities
- Venus envy; projects inner authority, beauty, and creativity onto others

Venus in Aquarius, Good Witch

- Experiments, individuates, explores who she is not in order to discover who she is
- Sexually and socially provocative
- Seeks beauty in diversity, authenticity, and truth
- Liberates people to be themselves by being authentic
- Acts of outrageousness/outrage are healing

Venus in Aquarius, Bad Witch

- Rebels against and can dissociate from her feminine, sensual side

- Can be difficult for her to get out of her head and into her body; may need to heal from abuse
- Suffers emotional disconnection in relationships
- Venus envy; attracted to rebels, geniuses, and progressives (because she is one!)

Venus in Pisces, Good Witch

- Generous with everything: affection, money, compassion, support, love
- Has eyes wide open to people who have emotional issues or a poor relationship to reality; learns to be discerning by using her sixth sense
- Shares spirituality and enchanted play with partners
- Regular retreat, solitude, and spiritual practice help her calm down and center

Venus in Pisces, Bad Witch

- Too easily overlooks red flags in others
- Just as the sea accepts and refuses no one, she is indiscriminately open to dating anyone
- Unconscious fantasy life can impede the practical checks and balances of a real relationship
- Unconsciously merges into another and loses herself

Appendix 2: Venus Tables, 1950 to 2020

Use these tables to find your Venus sign. First, find the table for your birth year. The dates on which Venus changed signs are listed. If you were born on a day when Venus changed signs, your Venus may be in the last degree of the prior sign, depending on your birth time zone. You will want to read the descriptors for both Venus signs, then choose the sign most fitting for you. Or visit the website www.astro.com and register your profile with your birth data. Select "Chart Drawing." Your Venus sign will appear in the box to the left.

1950	1951
Apr. 6–in Pisces	Jan. 7–in Aquarius
May 5–in Aries	Jan. 31–in Pisces
June 1–in Taurus	Feb. 24–in Aries
June 27–in Gemini	Mar. 21–in Taurus
July 22–in Cancer	Apr. 15–in Gemini
Aug. 16–in Leo	May 11–in Cancer
Sept. 10–in Virgo	June 7–in Leo
Oct. 4–in Libra	July 8–in Virgo
Oct. 28–in Scorpio	Nov. 9–in Libra
Nov. 21–in Sagittarius	Dec. 8–in Scorpio
Dec. 14–in Capricorn	
1952	**1953**
Jan. 2–in Sagittarius	Jan. 5–in Pisces
Jan. 27–in Capricorn	Feb. 2–in Aries
Feb. 21–in Aquarius	Mar. 14–in Taurus
Mar. 16–in Pisces	Mar. 31–in Aries
Apr. 9–in Aries	June 5–in Taurus
May 4–in Taurus	July 7–in Gemini
May 28–in Gemini	Aug. 4–in Cancer
June 22–in Cancer	Aug. 30–in Leo
July 16–in Leo	Sept. 24–in Virgo
Aug. 9–in Virgo	Oct. 18–in Libra
Sept. 3–in Libra	Nov. 11–in Scorpio
Sept. 27–in Scorpio	Dec. 5–in Sagittarius
Oct. 22–in Sagittarius	Dec. 29–in Capricorn
Nov. 15–in Capricorn	
Dec. 10–in Aquarius	

1954	1955
Jan. 22–in Aquarius	Jan. 6–in Sagittarius
Feb. 15–in Pisces	Feb. 6–in Capricorn
Mar. 11–in Aries	Mar. 4–in Aquarius
Apr. 4–in Taurus	Mar. 30–in Pisces
Apr. 28–in Gemini	Apr. 24–in Aries
May 23–in Cancer	May 19–in Taurus
June 17–in Leo	June 13–in Gemini
July 13–in Virgo	July 8–in Cancer
Aug. 9–in Libra	Aug. 1–in Leo
Sept. 6–in Scorpio	Aug. 25–in Virgo
Oct. 23–in Sagittarius	Sept. 18–in Libra
Oct. 27–in Scorpio	Oct. 13–in Scorpio
	Nov. 6–in Sagittarius
	Nov. 30–in Capricorn
	Dec. 24–in Aquarius

1956	1957
Jan. 17–in Pisces	Jan. 12–in Capricorn
Feb. 11–in Aries	Feb. 5–in Aquarius
Mar. 7–in Taurus	Mar. 1–in Pisces
Apr. 4–in Gemini	Mar. 25–in Aries
May 8–in Cancer	Apr. 19–in Taurus
June 23–in Gemini	May 13–in Gemini
Aug. 4–in Cancer	June 6–in Cancer
Sept. 8–in Leo	July 1–in Leo
Oct. 6–in Virgo	July 26–in Virgo
Oct. 31–in Libra	Aug. 20–in Libra
Nov. 25–in Scorpio	Sept. 14–in Scorpio
Dec. 19–in Sagittarius	Oct. 10–in Sagittarius
	Nov. 5–in Capricorn
	Dec. 6–in Aquarius

1958	1959
Apr. 6–in Pisces	Jan. 7–in Aquarius
May 5–in Aries	Jan. 31–in Pisces
June 1–in Taurus	Feb. 24–in Aries
June 26–in Gemini	Mar. 20–in Taurus
July 22–in Cancer	Apr. 14–in Gemini
Aug. 16–in Leo	May 10–in Cancer
Sept. 9–in Virgo	June 6–in Leo
Oct. 3–in Libra	July 8–in Virgo
Oct. 27–in Scorpio	Sept. 20–in Leo
Nov. 20–in Sagittarius	Dec. 14–in Capricorn
Dec. 14–in Capricorn	Sept. 25–in Virgo
	Nov. 9–in Libra
	Dec. 7–in Scorpio
1960	**1961**
Jan. 2–in Sagittarius	Jan. 5–in Pisces
Jan. 27–in Capricorn	Feb. 2–in Aries
Feb. 20–in Aquarius	June 5–in Taurus
Mar. 16–in Pisces	July 7–in Gemini
Apr. 9–in Aries	Aug. 3–in Cancer
May 3–in Taurus	Aug. 29–in Leo
May 28–in Gemini	Sept. 23–in Virgo
June 21–in Cancer	Oct. 18–in Libra
July 16–in Leo	Nov. 11–in Scorpio
Aug. 9–in Virgo	Dec. 5–in Sagittarius
Sept. 2–in Libra	Dec. 28–in Capricorn
Sept. 27–in Scorpio	
Oct. 21–in Sagittarius	
Nov. 15–in Capricorn	
Dec. 10–in Aquarius	

1962	1963
Jan. 21–in Aquarius	Jan. 6–in Sagittarius
Feb. 14–in Pisces	Feb. 5–in Capricorn
Mar. 10–in Aries	Mar. 4–in Aquarius
Apr. 3–in Taurus	Mar. 30–in Pisces
Apr. 28–in Gemini	Apr. 24–in Aries
May 23–in Cancer	May 19–in Taurus
June 17–in Leo	June 12–in Gemini
July 12–in Virgo	July 7–in Cancer
Aug. 8–in Libra	July 31–in Leo
Sept. 7–in Scorpio	Aug. 25–in Virgo
	Sept. 18–in Libra
	Oct. 12–in Scorpio
	Nov. 5–in Sagittarius
	Nov. 29–in Capricorn
	Dec. 23–in Aquarius
1964	**1965**
Jan. 17–in Pisces	Jan. 12–in Capricorn
Feb. 10–in Aries	Feb. 5–in Aquarius
Mar. 7–in Taurus	Mar. 1–in Pisces
Apr. 4–in Gemini	Mar. 25–in Aries
May 9–in Cancer	Apr. 18–in Taurus
June 17–in Gemini	May 12–in Gemini
Aug. 5–in Cancer	June 6–in Cancer
Sept. 8–in Leo	June 30–in Leo
Oct. 5–in Virgo	July 25–in Virgo
Oct. 31–in Libra	Aug. 20–in Libra
Nov. 25–in Scorpio	Sept. 13–in Scorpio
Dec. 19–in Sagittarius	Oct. 9–in Sagittarius
	Nov. 5–in Capricorn
	Dec. 7–in Aquarius

1966	1967
Feb. 6–in Capricorn	Jan. 6–in Aquarius
Feb. 25–in Aquarius	Jan. 30–in Pisces
Apr. 6–in Pisces	Feb. 23–in Aries
May 5–in Aries	Mar. 20–in Taurus
May 31–in Taurus	Apr. 14–in Gemini
June 26–in Gemini	May 10–in Cancer
July 21–in Cancer	June 6–in Leo
Aug. 15–in Leo	July 8–in Virgo
Sept. 8–in Virgo	Sept. 9–in Leo
Oct. 3–in Libra	Oct. 1–in Virgo
Oct. 27–in Scorpio	Nov. 9–in Libra
Nov. 20–in Sagittarius	Dec. 7–in Scorpio
Dec. 13–in Capricorn	
1968	**1969**
Jan. 1–in Sagittarius	Jan. 4–in Pisces
Jan. 26–in Capricorn	Feb. 2–in Aries
Feb. 20–in Aquarius	June 6–in Taurus
Mar. 15–in Pisces	July 6–in Gemini
Apr. 8–in Aries	Aug. 3–in Cancer
May 3–in Taurus	Aug. 29–in Leo
May 27–in Gemini	Sept. 23–in Virgo
June 21–in Cancer	Oct. 17–in Libra
July 15–in Leo	Nov. 10–in Scorpio
Aug. 8–in Virgo	Dec. 4–in Sagittarius
Sept. 2–in Libra	Dec. 28–in Capricorn
Sept. 26–in Scorpio	
Oct. 21–in Sagittarius	
Nov. 14–in Capricorn	
Dec. 9–in Aquarius	

1970	1971
Jan. 21–in Aquarius	Jan. 7–in Sagittarius
Feb. 14–in Pisces	Feb. 5–in Capricorn
Mar. 10–in Aries	Mar. 4–in Aquarius
Apr. 3–in Taurus	Mar. 29–in Pisces
Apr. 27–in Gemini	Apr. 23–in Aries
May 22–in Cancer	May 18–in Taurus
June 16–in Leo	June 12–in Gemini
July 12–in Virgo	July 6–in Cancer
Aug. 8–in Libra	July 31–in Leo
Sept. 7–in Scorpio	Aug. 24–in Virgo
	Sept. 17–in Libra
	Oct. 11–in Scorpio
	Nov. 5–in Sagittarius
	Nov. 29–in Capricorn
	Dec. 23–in Aquarius
1972	**1973**
Jan. 16–in Pisces	Jan. 11–in Capricorn
Feb. 10–in Aries	Feb. 4–in Aquarius
Mar. 7–in Taurus	Feb. 28–in Pisces
Apr. 3–in Gemini	Mar. 24–in Aries
May 10–in Cancer	Apr. 18–in Taurus
June 11–in Gemini	May 12–in Gemini
Aug. 6–in Cancer	June 5–in Cancer
Sept. 7–in Leo	June 30–in Leo
Oct. 5–in Virgo	July 25–in Virgo
Oct. 30–in Libra	Aug. 19–in Libra
Nov. 24–in Scorpio	Sept. 13–in Scorpio
Dec. 18–in Sagittarius	Oct. 9–in Sagittarius
	Nov. 5–in Capricorn
	Dec. 7–in Aquarius

1974	1975
Jan. 29–Capricorn	Jan. 6–in Aquarius
Feb. 28–in Aquarius	Jan. 30–in Pisces
Apr. 6–in Pisces	Feb. 23–in Aries
May 4–in Aries	Mar. 19–in Taurus
May 31–in Taurus	Apr. 13–in Gemini
June 25–in Gemini	May 9–in Cancer
July 21–in Cancer	June 6–in Leo
Aug. 14–in Leo	July 9–in Virgo
Sept. 8–in Virgo	Sept. 2–in Leo
Oct. 2–in Libra	Oct. 4–in Virgo
Oct. 26–in Scorpio	Nov. 9–in Libra
Nov. 19–in Sagittarius	Dec. 7–in Scorpio
Dec. 13–in Capricorn	
1976	**1977**
Jan. 1–in Sagittarius	Jan. 4–in Pisces
Jan. 26–in Capricorn	Feb. 2–in Aries
Feb. 19–in Aquarius	June 6–in Taurus
Mar. 15–in Pisces	July 6–in Gemini
Apr. 8–in Aries	Aug. 2–in Cancer
May 2–in Taurus	Aug. 28–in Leo
May 27–in Gemini	Sept. 22–in Virgo
June 20–in Cancer	Oct. 17–in Libra
July 14–in Leo	Nov. 10–in Scorpio
Aug. 8–in Virgo	Dec. 4–in Sagittarius
Sept. 1–in Libra	Dec. 27–in Capricorn
Sept. 26–in Scorpio	
Oct. 20–in Sagittarius	
Nov. 14–in Capricorn	
Dec. 9–in Aquarius	

1978	1979
Jan. 20–in Aquarius	Jan. 7–in Sagittarius
Feb. 13–in Pisces	Feb. 5–in Capricorn
Mar. 9–in Aries	Mar. 3–in Aquarius
Apr. 2–in Taurus	Mar. 29–in Pisces
Apr. 27–in Gemini	Apr. 23–in Aries
May 22–in Cancer	May 18–in Taurus
June 16–in Leo	June 11–in Gemini
July 12–in Virgo	July 6–in Cancer
Aug. 8–in Libra	July 30–in Leo
Sept. 7–in Scorpio	Aug. 24–in Virgo
	Sept. 17–in Libra
	Oct. 11–in Scorpio
	Nov. 4–in Sagittarius
	Nov. 28–in Capricorn
	Dec. 22–in Aquarius
1980	**1981**
Jan. 16–in Pisces	Jan. 11–in Capricorn
Feb. 9–in Aries	Feb. 4–in Aquarius
Mar. 6–in Taurus	Feb. 28–in Pisces
Apr. 3–in Gemini	Mar. 24–in Aries
May 12–in Cancer	Apr. 17–in Taurus
June 5–in Gemini	May 11–in Gemini
Aug. 6–in Cancer	June 5–in Cancer
Sept. 7–in Leo	June 29–in Leo
Oct. 4–in Virgo	July 24–in Virgo
Oct. 30–in Libra	Aug. 18–in Libra
Nov. 24–in Scorpio	Sept. 12–in Scorpio
Dec. 18–in Sagittarius	Oct. 9–in Sagittarius
	Nov. 5–in Capricorn
	Dec. 8–in Aquarius

1982	1983
Jan. 23–in Capricorn	Jan. 5–in Aquarius
Mar. 2–in Aquarius	Jan. 29–in Pisces
Apr. 6–in Pisces	Feb. 22–in Aries
May 4–in Aries	Mar. 19–in Taurus
May 30–in Taurus	Apr. 13–in Gemini
June 25–in Gemini	May 9–in Cancer
July 20–in Cancer	June 6–in Leo
Aug. 14–in Leo	July 10–in Virgo
Sept. 7–in Virgo	Aug. 27–in Leo
Oct. 2–in Libra	Oct. 5–in Virgo
Oct. 26–in Scorpio	Nov. 9–in Libra
Nov. 18–in Sagittarius	Dec. 6–in Scorpio
Dec. 12–in Capricorn	

1984	1985
Jan. 1–in Sagittarius	Jan. 4–in Pisces
Jan. 25–in Capricorn	Feb. 2–in Aries
Feb. 19–in Aquarius	June 6–in Taurus
Mar. 14–in Pisces	July 6–in Gemini
Apr. 7–in Aries	Aug. 2–in Cancer
May 2–in Taurus	Aug. 28–in Leo
May 28–in Gemini	Sept. 22–in Virgo
June 20–in Cancer	Oct. 16–in Libra
July 14–in Leo	Nov. 9–in Scorpio
Aug. 7–in Virgo	Dec. 3–in Sagittarius
Sept. 1–in Libra	Dec. 27–in Capricorn
Sept. 25–in Scorpio	
Oct. 20–in Sagittarius	
Nov. 13–in Capricorn	
Dec. 9–in Aquarius	

1986	1987
Jan. 20–in Aquarius	Jan. 7–in Sagittarius
Feb. 13–in Pisces	Feb. 5–in Capricorn
Mar. 9–in Aries	Mar. 3–in Aquarius
Apr. 2–in Taurus	Mar. 28–in Pisces
Apr. 26–in Gemini	Apr. 22–in Aries
May 21–in Cancer	May 17–in Taurus
June 15–in Leo	June 11–in Gemini
July 11–in Virgo	July 5–in Cancer
Aug. 7–in Libra	July 30–in Leo
Sept. 7–in Scorpio	Aug. 23–in Virgo
	Sept. 16–in Libra
	Oct. 10–in Scorpio
	Nov. 3–in Sagittarius
	Nov. 28–in Capricorn
	Dec. 22–in Aquarius
1988	**1989**
Jan. 15–in Pisces	Jan. 10–in Capricorn
Feb. 9–in Aries	Feb. 3–in Aquarius
Mar. 6–in Taurus	Feb. 27–in Pisces
Apr. 3–in Gemini	Mar. 23–in Aries
May 17–in Cancer	Apr. 16–in Taurus
May 27–in Gemini	May 1–in Gemini
Aug. 6–in Cancer	June 4–in Cancer
Sept. 7–in Leo	June 29–in Leo
Oct. 4–in Virgo	July 24–in Virgo
Oct. 29–in Libra	Aug. 18–in Libra
Nov. 23–in Scorpio	Sept. 12–in Scorpio
Dec. 17–in Sagittarius	Oct. 8–in Sagittarius
	Nov. 5–in Capricorn
	Dec. 10–in Aquarius

1990	1991
Jan. 16–in Capricorn	Jan. 5–in Aquarius
Mar. 3–in Aquarius	Jan. 29–in Pisces
Apr. 6–in Pisces	Feb. 22–in Aries
May 4–in Aries	Mar. 18–in Taurus
May 30–in Taurus	Apr. 13–in Gemini
June 25–in Gemini	May 9–in Cancer
July 20–in Cancer	June 6–in Leo
Aug. 13–in Leo	July 11–in Virgo
Sept. 7–in Virgo	Aug. 21–in Leo
Oct. 1–in Libra	Oct. 6–in Virgo
Oct. 25–in Scorpio	Nov. 9–in Libra
Nov. 18–in Sagittarius	Dec. 6–in Scorpio
Dec. 12–in Capricorn	Dec. 31–in Sagittarius
1992	**1993**
Jan. 25–in Capricorn	Jan. 3–in Pisces
Feb. 18–in Aquarius	Feb. 2–in Aries
Mar. 13–in Pisces	June 6–in Taurus
Apr. 7–in Aries	July 6–in Gemini
May 1–in Taurus	Aug. 1–in Cancer
May 26–in Gemini	Aug. 27–in Leo
June 19–in Cancer	Sept. 21–in Virgo
July 13–in Leo	Oct. 16–in Libra
Aug. 7–in Virgo	Nov. 9–in Scorpio
Aug. 31–in Libra	Dec. 2–in Sagittarius
Sept. 25–in Scorpio	Dec. 26–in Capricorn
Oct. 19–in Sagittarius	
Nov. 13–in Capricorn	
Dec. 8–in Aquarius	

1994	1995
Jan. 19–in Aquarius	Jan. 7–in Sagittarius
Feb. 12–in Pisces	Feb. 4–in Capricorn
Mar. 8–in Aries	Mar. 2–in Aquarius
Apr. 1–in Taurus	Mar. 28–in Pisces
Apr. 26–in Gemini	Apr. 22–in Aries
May 21–in Cancer	May 16–in Taurus
June 15–in Leo	June 10–in Gemini
July 11–in Virgo	July 5–in Cancer
Aug. 7–in Libra	July 29–in Leo
Sept. 7–in Scorpio	Aug. 23–in Virgo
Oct. 4–in Leo	Sept. 16–in Libra
Dec. 12–in Virgo	Oct. 10–in Scorpio
	Nov. 3–in Sagittarius
	Nov. 27–in Capricorn
	Dec. 21–in Aquarius

1996	1997
Jan. 15–in Pisces	Jan. 10–in Capricorn
Feb. 9–in Aries	Feb. 3–in Aquarius
Mar. 6–in Taurus	Feb. 27–in Pisces
Apr. 3–in Gemini	Mar. 23–in Aries
Aug. 7–in Cancer	Apr. 16–in Taurus
Sept. 7–in Leo	May 10–in Gemini
Oct. 4–in Virgo	June 4–in Cancer
Oct. 29–in Libra	June 28–in Leo
Nov. 23–in Scorpio	July 23–in Virgo
Dec. 17–in Sagittarius	Aug. 17–in Libra
	Sept. 12–in Scorpio
	Oct. 8–in Sagittarius
	Nov. 5–in Capricorn
	Dec. 12–in Aquarius

1998	1999
Jan. 9–in Capricorn	Jan. 4–in Aquarius
Mar. 4–in Aquarius	Jan. 28–in Pisces
Apr. 6–in Pisces	Feb. 21–in Aries
May 3–in Aries	Mar. 18–in Taurus
May 29–in Taurus	Apr. 12–in Gemini
June 24–in Gemini	May 8–in Cancer
July 19–in Cancer	June 5–in Leo
Aug. 13–in Leo	July 12–in Virgo
Sept. 6–in Virgo	Aug. 15–in Leo
Sept. 30–in Libra	Oct. 7–in Virgo
Oct. 24–in Scorpio	Nov. 9–in Libra
Nov. 17–in Sagittarius	Dec. 5–in Scorpio
Dec. 11–in Capricorn	Dec. 31–in Sagittarius
2000	**2001**
Jan. 24–in Capricorn	Jan. 3–in Pisces
Feb. 18–in Aquarius	Feb. 2–in Aries
Mar. 13–in Pisces	June 6–in Taurus
Apr. 6–in Aries	July 5–in Gemini
May 1–in Taurus	Aug. 1–in Cancer
May 25–in Gemini	Aug. 27–in Leo
June 18–in Cancer	Sept. 21–in Virgo
July 13–in Leo	Oct. 15–in Libra
Aug. 6–in Virgo	Nov. 8–in Scorpio
Aug. 31–in Libra	Dec. 2–in Sagittarius
Sept. 24–in Scorpio	Dec. 26–in Capricorn
Oct. 19–in Sagittarius	
Nov. 13–in Capricorn	
Dec. 8–in Aquarius	

2002	2003
Jan. 19–in Aquarius	Jan. 7–in Sagittarius
Feb. 12–in Pisces	Feb. 4–in Capricorn
Mar. 8–in Aries	Mar. 2–in Aquarius
Apr. 1–in Taurus	Mar. 27–in Pisces
Apr. 25–in Gemini	Apr. 21–in Aries
May 20–in Cancer	May 16–in Taurus
June 14–in Leo	June 10–in Gemini
July 10–in Virgo	July 4–in Cancer
Aug. 7–in Libra	July 29–in Leo
Sept. 8–in Scorpio	Aug. 22–in Virgo
	Sept. 15–in Libra
	Oct. 9–in Scorpio
	Nov. 2–in Sagittarius
	Nov. 27–in Capricorn
	Dec. 21–in Aquarius
2004	**2005**
Jan. 14–in Pisces	Jan. 9–in Capricorn
Feb. 8–in Aries	Feb. 2–in Aquarius
Mar. 5–in Taurus	Feb. 26–in Pisces
Apr. 3–in Gemini	Mar. 22–in Aries
Aug. 7–in Cancer	Apr. 15–in Taurus
Sept. 6–in Leo	May 10–in Gemini
Oct. 3–in Virgo	June 3–in Cancer
Oct. 29–in Libra	June 28–in Leo
Nov. 22–in Scorpio	July 23–in Virgo
Dec. 16–in Sagittarius	Aug. 17–in Libra
	Sept. 11–in Scorpio
	Oct. 8–in Sagittarius
	Nov. 5–in Capricorn
	Dec. 15–in Aquarius

2006	2007
Jan. 1–in Capricorn	Jan. 4–in Aquarius
Mar. 5–in Aquarius	Jan. 28–in Pisces
Apr. 6–in Pisces	Feb. 21–in Aries
May 3–in Aries	Mar. 17–in Taurus
May 29–in Taurus	Apr. 12–in Gemini
June 24–in Gemini	May 8–in Cancer
July 19–in Cancer	June 5–in Leo
Aug. 12–in Leo	July 14–in Virgo
Sept. 6–in Virgo	Aug. 9–in Leo
Oct. 24–in Scorpio	Oct. 8–in Virgo
Nov. 17–in Sagittarius	Nov. 8–in Libra
Dec. 11–in Capricorn	Dec. 5–in Scorpio
	Dec. 30–in Sagittarius
2008	**2009**
Jan. 24–in Capricorn	Jan. 3–in Pisces
Feb. 17–in Aquarius	Feb. 3–in Aries
Mar. 12–in Pisces	Apr. 11–in Pisces
Apr. 6–in Aries	Apr. 24–in Aries
Apr. 30–in Taurus	June 6–in Taurus
May 24–in Gemini	July 5–in Gemini
June 18–in Cancer	Aug. 1–in Cancer
July 12–in Leo	Aug. 26–in Leo
Aug. 6–in Virgo	Sept. 20–in Virgo
Aug. 29–in Libra	Oct. 14–in Libra
Sept. 24–in Scorpio	Nov. 8–in Scorpio
Oct. 18–in Sagittarius	Dec. 1–in Sagittarius
Nov. 12–in Capricorn	Dec. 25–in Capricorn
Dec. 7–in Aquarius	

2010	2011
Jan. 18–in Aquarius	Jan. 8–in Sagittarius
Feb. 11–in Pisces	Feb. 5–in Capricorn
Mar. 7–in Aries	Mar. 3–in Aquarius
Mar. 31–in Taurus	Mar. 28–in Pisces
Apr. 25–in Gemini	Apr. 22–in Aries
May 20–in Cancer	May 16–in Taurus
June 14–in Leo	Jun. 10–in Gemini
July 10–in Virgo	Jul. 5–in Cancer
Aug. 7–in Libra	Jul. 29–in Leo
Sept. 8–in Scorpio	Aug. 22–in Virgo
Nov. 8–in Libra	Sep.16–in Libra
Nov. 30–in Scorpio	Oct. 10–in Scorpio
	Nov. 3–in Sagittarius
	Nov. 27–in Capricorn
	Dec. 21–in Aquarius
2012	**2013**
Jan. 15–in Pisces	Jan. 10–in Capricorn
Feb. 9–in Aries	Feb. 3–in Aquarius
Mar. 6–in Taurus	Feb. 27–in Pisces
Apr. 4–in Gemini	Mar. 23–in Aries
Aug. 8–in Cancer	Apr. 16–in Taurus
Sep. 7–in Leo	May 10–in Gemini
Oct. 4–in Virgo	Jun. 4–in Cancer
Oct. 29–in Libra	Jun. 28–in Leo
Nov. 23–in Scorpio	Jul. 23–in Virgo
Dec. 17–in Sagittarius	Aug 17–in Libra
	Sept. 12–in Scorpio
	Oct. 8–in Sagittarius
	Nov. 6–in Capricorn

2014	2015
Mar. 6–in Aquarius	Jan. 4–in Aquarius
Apr. 6–in Pisces	Jan. 28–in Pisces
May 4–in Aries	Feb. 21–in Aries
May 30–in Taurus	Mar. 18–in Taurus
Jun. 24–in Gemini	Apr. 12–in Gemini
Jul. 19–in Cancer	May 8–in Cancer
Aug. 13–in Leo	Jun. 6–in Leo
Sep. 6–in Virgo	Jul. 19– in Virgo
Sep. 30–in Libra	Aug. 1–in Leo
Oct. 24–in Scorpio	Oct. 9–in Virgo
Nov. 17–in Sagittarius	Nov. 9–in Libra
Dec. 11–in Capricorn	Dec. 6–in Scorpio
	Dec. 31–in Sagittarius
2016	**2017**
Jan. 24–in Capricorn	Jan. 4–in Pisces
Feb. 18–in Aquarius	Feb. 4–in Aries
Mar. 13–in Pisces	Apr. 4–in Pisces
Apr. 6–in Aries	Apr. 29–in Aries
May 1–in Taurus	Jun 7–in Taurus
May 25 in Gemini	Jul 6–in Gemini
Jun 18–in Cancer	Aug. 1–in Cancer
Jul. 13–in Leo	Aug. 27–in Leo
Aug. 6–in Virgo	Sep. 21–in Virgo
Aug. 31–in Libra	Oct. 15–in Libra
Sep. 24–in Scorpio	Nov. 8–in Scorpio
Oct. 19–in Sagittarius	Dec. 2–in Sagittarius
Nov. 13–in Capricorn	Dec. 26–in Capricorn
Dec. 8–in Aquarius	

2018	2019
Jan. 19–in Aquarius	Jan 8–in Sagittarius
Feb. 11–in Pisces	Feb. 4–in Capricorn
Mar. 7–in Aries	Mar. 2–in Aquarius
Apr. 1–in Taurus	Mar. 27–in Pisces
Apr. 25–in Gemini	Apr. 21–in Aries
May 20–in Cancer	May 16–in Taurus
Jun 14–in Leo	Jun. 10–in Gemini
Jul. 11–in Virgo	Jul. 4–in Cancer
Aug. 7–in Libra	Jul. 29–in Leo
Sep. 10–in Scorpio	Aug. 22–in Virgo
Nov. 1–in Libra	Sep. 15–in Libra
Dec. 3–in Scorpio	Oct. 9–in Scorpio
	Nov. 2–in Sagittarius
	Nov. 27–in Capricorn
	Dec. 21–in Aquarius

2020	Notes
Jan. 14–in Pisces	
Feb. 8–in Aries	
Mar. 6–in Taurus	
Apr. 4–in Gemini	
Aug. 8–in Cancer	
Sep. 7–in Leo	
Oct. 3–in Virgo	
Oct. 29–in Libra	
Nov. 22–in Scorpio	
Dec. 16–in Sagittarius	

To Write to the Author

If you wish to contact the author or would like more information about this book, please write to the author in care of Llewellyn Worldwide Ltd. and we will forward your request. Both the author and publisher appreciate hearing from you and learning of your enjoyment of this book and how it has helped you. Llewellyn Worldwide Ltd. cannot guarantee that every letter written to the author can be answered, but all will be forwarded. Please write to:

Jessica Shepherd
℅ Llewellyn Worldwide
2143 Wooddale Drive
Woodbury, MN 55125-2989

Please enclose a self-addressed stamped envelope for reply, or $1.00 to cover costs. If outside the U.S.A., enclose an international postal reply coupon.

Many of Llewellyn's authors have websites with additional information and resources.
For more information,
please visit our website at www.llewellyn.com.